W9-BLC-839

VOLUME 1

DIABETIC LIVING™ EVERYDAY COOKING IS
PART OF A BOOK SERIES PUBLISHED BY
BETTER HOMES AND GARDENS SPECIAL
INTEREST MEDIA, DES MOINES, IOWA

Summer Berry Panna Cotta
recipe, page 138

(letter from the editor)

Getting a nutritious meal on the table for our family is a health-smart daily goal for many of us. When you or someone in your family has diabetes, healthful eating has to be a priority. But it's not always easy. I know because I have had type 1 diabetes since I was 4.

Like many couples, my husband, Mark, and I both work. So preparing satisfying fare that is nutritionally sound and workable with my diabetes meal plan is often a struggle. It becomes even more challenging when you add a 10-year-old boy to the mix! My son, Grant, likes to help in the kitchen. And he has learned to like foods that many kids wouldn't, such as polenta, salmon, and Brussels sprouts. OK, maybe Brussels sprouts not so much. But our rule is for him to try one bite of any new recipe, which exposes him to different foods and flavors. I hope your family will enjoy trying new tastes using the familiar and perhaps not-so-familiar ingredients in these recipes. Each one is approved by our Test Kitchen as delicious, nutritious, and easy to make.

Sunday evening is my big night to cook several dinners for the week. That's why I love the make-ahead directions we've included with many of the recipes. You can have the dishes in the "Family-Pleasing Meals" chapter on the table in 30 minutes or less. We've also included a few slow-cooker recipes. A cookbook that keeps your meal plan goals in line and includes nutrition information is a real help in managing your diabetes. I look forward to serving recipes from this cookbook and hope you and your family will enjoy them, too!

Kelly Rawlings

Kelly Rawlings, editor
Diabetic Living® magazine

ON THE COVER: Basil-Lemon Shrimp Linguine (recipe, page 32).
Photographer: Blaine Moats.
Food stylist: Dianna Nolin.

Editorial Director JOHN RIHA
Creative Director BRIDGET SANDQUIST

Editor KELLY RAWLINGS
Design Director TED ROSSITER

Contributing Editor KRISTI THOMAS, R.D.
Interactive Editor RACHEL MARTIN
Contributing Copy Editor GRETCHEN KAUFFMAN
Contributing Proofreader CARRIE SCHMITZ
Test Kitchen Director LYNN BLANCHARD
Test Kitchen Product Supervisor LAURA MARZEN, R.D.
Editorial Assistants MARLENE TODD, SHERI CORD
Business Office Assistant SHARON LEIN

Deputy Art Director MICHELLE BILYEU
Assistant Art Director JEN REDMOND
Contributing Designer JILL BUDDEN
Interactive Designer RACHEL DIERENFIELD

EDITORIAL ADMINISTRATION

Managing Editor KATHLEEN ARMENTROUT
Copy Chief DOUG KOUMA
Office Manager CINDY SLOBASZEWSKI
Senior Copy Editors ELIZABETH KEEST SEDREL, JENNIFER SPEER RAMUNDT

EDITORIAL SERVICES

Color/Quality Manager DALE TUNENDER
Photo Studio Manager JEFF ANDERSON
Color/Quality Analyst HEIDI PARCEL
Prepress Desktop Specialist KRISTIN E. REESE

CONSUMER MARKETING

Vice President, Consumer Marketing DAVE BALL
Consumer Products Marketing Director STEVE SWANSON
Consumer Products Marketing Manager WENDY MERICAL
Business Director JIM LEONARD
Production Director DOUGLAS M. JOHNSTON
Book Production Manager MARJORIE J. SCHENKELBERG

MEREDITH PUBLISHING GROUP

President JACK GRIFFIN
President, Better Homes and Gardens ANDY SAREYAN
Editorial Director MIKE LAFAVORE **Finance and Administration** MIKE RIGGS
Manufacturing BRUCE HESTON **Corporate Sales** JACK BAMBERGER
Interactive Media LAUREN WIENER **Corporate Marketing** NANCY WEBER
Research BRITTA WARE **Chief Technology Officer** TINA STEIL
New Media Marketing Services ANDY WILSON

President and Chief Executive Officer STEPHEN M. LACY

Chairman of the Board WILLIAM T. KERR

In Memoriam — E.T. MEREDITH III (1933-2003)

Diabetic Living Everyday Cooking is part of a series published by Meredith Corp., 1716 Locust St., Des Moines, IA 50309-3023.

If you have comments or questions about the editorial material in *Diabetic Living Everyday Cooking,* write to the editor of *Diabetic Living* magazine, Meredith Corp., 1716 Locust St., Des Moines, IA 50309-3023. Send an e-mail to diabeticliving@meredith.com or call 800/678-2651. *Diabetic Living* magazine is available by subscription or on the newsstand. To order a subscription to *Diabetic Living* magazine, go to *DiabeticLivingOnline.com.*

First edition. Printed in U.S.A.

ISBN 978-0-696-24147-5

contents

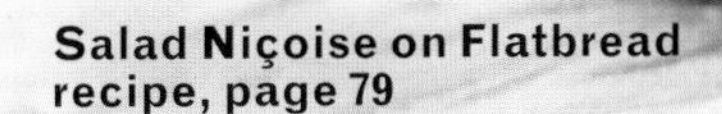

Salad Niçoise on Flatbread
recipe, page 79

family-pleasing dinners

Thai Pork Stir-Fry

If you think tasty meals are hard to serve during the week, turn to these family-favorite dishes. From poultry and pork to beef or fish, our recipes will help you prepare healthful dinners on busy days in 30 minutes or less.

Thai Pork Stir-Fry

Grate or cut off what you need, then freeze any leftover unpeeled fresh ginger.

PER SERVING: 301 cal., 11 g total fat (3 g sat. fat), 71 mg chol., 206 mg sodium, 21 g carb., 3 g fiber, 28 g pro. Exchanges: 1 vegetable, 1 starch, 3 lean meat, 1 fat. Carb choices: 1.5.

2 tablespoons olive oil
1 tablespoon reduced-sodium soy sauce
½ teaspoon garlic powder
½ teaspoon ground cardamom
½ teaspoon chili powder
½ teaspoon ground black pepper
½ teaspoon finely chopped fresh ginger or ¼ teaspoon ground ginger
1½ pounds boneless pork loin, cut into bite-size strips
2 cups broccoli florets
1 cup thinly sliced carrots
1 cup cauliflower florets
2 tablespoons white vinegar
1 tablespoon curry powder
2 cups hot cooked brown rice

1. In a very large skillet, combine oil, soy sauce, garlic powder, cardamom, chili powder, pepper, and ginger. Add half of the pork.

2. Stir-fry pork over medium-high heat for 3 minutes. Using a slotted spoon, remove pork from skillet. Repeat with the remaining pork. Return all of the pork to the skillet.

3. Add broccoli, carrots, cauliflower, vinegar, and curry powder to pork mixture. Bring to boiling; reduce heat. Cover and simmer pork and vegetables for 3 to 5 minutes or until vegetables are crisp-tender, stirring occasionally. Serve over hot cooked brown rice. Makes 6 servings (1 cup stir-fry and ⅓ cup rice each).

(label lingo)

To keep your nutrition goals in check, learn to read labels. The "nutrition facts" label helps you track how much fat, saturated fat, cholesterol, sodium, fiber, and important nutrients you eat. The label also lists the number of calories and grams of carbohydrates, protein, and fat in a serving. You can use these numbers to calculate exchanges. Some food manufacturers list exchanges on the package. All recipes in this book also list nutrition facts and exchanges. Supermarkets often display nutrition information for fresh meat, poultry, seafood, vegetables, and fruits on posters or offer take-home brochures for consumers.

Pork Chops with Red Cabbage and Pears

Cranberry Pork Loin Chops

Cranberry Pork Loin Chops

Ladle the tangy orange-and-cranberry sauce onto broiled or grilled chicken and fish, too.

PER SERVING: 285 cal., 7 g total fat (2 g sat. fat), 89 mg chol., 172 mg sodium, 21 g carb., 1 g fiber, 31 g pro. Exchanges: 1.5 carb., 4 lean meat. Carb choices: 1.5.

Nonstick cooking spray
4 boneless pork loin chops, cut ½ inch thick (about 1¼ pounds total)
½ cup canned whole cranberry sauce
2 tablespoons frozen orange juice concentrate, thawed
1 tablespoon honey
¼ teaspoon ground ginger
⅛ teaspoon ground nutmeg

1. Lightly coat an unheated large nonstick skillet with cooking spray. Preheat over medium-high heat. Sprinkle all sides of the chops with ⅛ teaspoon *salt* and ⅛ teaspoon ground *black pepper.* Add chops to hot skillet; reduce heat to medium. Cook for 8 to 10 minutes or until done (160°F), turning once. Remove chops from skillet; cover to keep warm.

2. Meanwhile, combine cranberry sauce, juice concentrate, honey, ginger, and nutmeg. Add mixture to same skillet. Cook and stir for 1 to 2 minutes or until slightly thickened. Serve over chops. Makes 4 servings.

Pork Chops with Red Cabbage and Pears

The sweet-and-sour cabbage pairs deliciously with braised chops.

PER SERVING: 239 cal., 4 g total fat (1 g sat. fat), 70 mg chol., 323 mg sodium, 20 g carb., 4 g fiber, 30 g pro. Exchanges: 1 vegetable, 0.5 fruit, 0.5 carb., 4 very lean meat. Carb choices: 1.

PER SERVING WITH SUBSTITUTE: same as above, except 222 cal., 15 g carb. Exchanges: 0 carb. Carb choices: 0.

¼ cup cider vinegar
2 tablespoons packed brown sugar or brown sugar substitute* equivalent to 2 tablespoons brown sugar
½ teaspoon dried sage, crushed
6 small pork loin chops, cut ½ inch thick (about 2 pounds total)**
½ teaspoon dried thyme, crushed
¼ teaspoon salt
⅛ teaspoon ground black pepper
2 teaspoons canola oil
6 cups coarsely shredded red cabbage
1 cup sliced onion
2 medium pears, cored and sliced
Snipped fresh sage and/or thyme (optional)

1. In a small bowl, combine cider vinegar, brown sugar, and ¼ teaspoon of the sage. Reserve 1 tablespoon of the mixture; set aside.

2. Sprinkle chops with dried thyme, salt, remaining ¼ teaspoon sage, and pepper. In a large skillet, heat oil over medium-high heat. Add chops. Cook for 6 to 8 minutes or until pork is slightly pink in the center and juices run clear (160°F), turning pork chops once halfway through cooking and brushing with 1 tablespoon vinegar mixture for the last 1 minute of cooking. Remove pork chops from skillet; cover and keep warm.

3. Add red cabbage and onion to skillet. Cook and stir over medium-high heat for 6 minutes. Add the reserved vinegar mixture and pears to skillet. Bring to boiling; reduce heat. Cover and simmer for 5 minutes. Top with pork chops; heat through. If desired, sprinkle chops with fresh sage and/or thyme. Makes 6 servings (1 chop and scant 1 cup cabbage mixture each).

***Sugar Substitutes:** Choose from Sweet'N Low Brown or Sugar Twin Granulated Brown. Follow package directions to use product amount equivalent to 2 tablespoons brown sugar.

****Test Kitchen Tip:** To keep the sodium in this dish in check, look for natural pork, not enhanced pork.

Adobo Pork Chops

Adobo is the Spanish word for seasoning or marinade. This chili-spiced version also has a smidgen of cinnamon.

PER SERVING: 189 cal., 7 g total fat (2 g sat. fat), 71 mg chol., 170 mg sodium, 3 g carb., 0 g fiber, 25 g pro. Exchanges: 4 very lean meat, 1 fat. Carb choices: 0.

- **6 boneless pork top loin chops, cut ¾ inch thick**
- **2 tablespoons packed brown sugar**
- **2 tablespoons olive oil**
- **2 tablespoons orange juice**
- **2 tablespoons snipped fresh cilantro**
- **1 tablespoon red wine vinegar or cider vinegar**
- **2 teaspoons chili powder**
- **1 teaspoon ground cumin**
- **1 teaspoon dried oregano, crushed**
- **¼ teaspoon cayenne pepper (optional)**
- **¼ teaspoon ground cinnamon**
- **3 cloves garlic, minced**
- **½ teaspoon salt**

1. Place chops in resealable plastic bag set in a shallow dish. In a bowl, combine remaining ingredients; pour over chops. Seal bag; turn to coat. Marinate in refrigerator for 2 to 24 hours.

2. Drain chops; discard marinade. Grill on rack of an uncovered grill directly over medium heat for 12 to 15 minutes or until medium doneness (160°F), turning once. Makes 6 servings.

Adobo Pork Chops

Pork Medaillons with Lemon-Pecan Spinach

Zippy spinach replaces the usual starchy vegetable.

PER SERVING: 213 cal., 10 g total fat (2 g sat. fat), 73 mg chol., 318 mg sodium, 5 g carb., 3 g fiber, 27 g pro. Exchanges: 1 vegetable, 3.5 lean meat, 0.5 fat. Carb choices: 0.

- **1 pound pork tenderloin, cut crosswise into 8 slices**
- **¼ teaspoon salt**
- **¼ teaspoon coarsely ground black pepper**
- **1 tablespoon canola oil or margarine**
- **2 tablespoons lemon juice**
- **⅛ teaspoon bottled hot pepper sauce**
- **1 10-ounce package frozen chopped spinach, thawed and well-drained**
- **2 green onions, sliced**
- **2 tablespoons chopped pecans**
- **1 tablespoon snipped fresh parsley**
- **⅛ teaspoon salt**
- **Lemon slices, halved (optional)**

1. If necessary, press each pork tenderloin slice to 1-inch thickness. Sprinkle pork slices lightly with the ¼ teaspoon salt and pepper.

2. In a large skillet, heat oil over medium-high heat. Add pork slices; cook for 6 to 8 minutes or until pork is slightly pink in the center (160°F), turning once halfway through cooking. Remove pork from skillet, reserving drippings in the skillet. Cover pork and keep warm.

3. Stir lemon juice and hot pepper sauce into reserved drippings in skillet. Stir in spinach, green onions, pecans, parsley, and the ⅛ teaspoon salt. Cook over low heat until spinach mixture is heated through.

4. Place spinach mixture on a platter; arrange pork slices on top. If desired, garnish with lemon slices. Makes 4 servings.

Quick Tip:

Some cuts of pork compare favorably with the white meat of chicken. A 3-ounce portion of roasted pork tenderloin, for example, has 139 calories and 4 grams of fat. The same size portion of roasted chicken (breast meat, no skin) has 142 calories and 3 grams of fat.

Pork Medaillons with Lemon-Pecan Spinach

Sesame Orange Beef

Sesame Orange Beef

For a triple hit of orange bliss, use orange juice, peel, and slices in this lighter version of the Asian classic.

PER SERVING: 348 cal., 10 g total fat (2 g sat. fat), 52 mg chol., 341 mg sodium, 41 g carb., 6 g fiber, 24 g pro. Exchanges: 1 vegetable, 1 fruit, 1.5 starch, 2.5 lean meat. Carb choices: 3.

8 ounces fresh green beans, halved crosswise
2 teaspoons sesame seeds
½ teaspoon finely shredded orange peel
½ cup orange juice
2 tablespoons reduced-sodium soy sauce
1 tablespoon toasted sesame oil
1 teaspoon cornstarch
Nonstick cooking spray
½ cup bias-sliced green onions
1 tablespoon grated fresh ginger
2 cloves garlic, minced
1 teaspoon cooking oil
12 ounces boneless beef sirloin steak, thinly sliced
2 cups hot cooked brown rice
2 oranges, peeled and thinly sliced crosswise or sectioned

1. In a covered medium saucepan, cook green beans in a small amount of boiling water for 6 to 8 minutes or until crisp-tender. Drain; set aside.

2. Meanwhile, in a small skillet, toast sesame seeds over medium heat for 1 to 2 minutes, stirring frequently. Set aside.

3. For sauce, in a small bowl, combine orange peel, orange juice, soy sauce, toasted sesame oil, and cornstarch; set aside.

4. Coat an unheated large nonstick skillet with cooking spray. Preheat over medium-high heat. Add green onions, ginger, and garlic to hot skillet; cook and stir for 1 minute. Add the precooked green beans; cook and stir for 2 minutes. Remove vegetables from skillet.

5. Carefully add cooking oil to the hot skillet. Add beef; cook and stir about 3 minutes or until desired doneness. Remove beef from skillet.

6. Stir sauce; add to skillet. Cook and stir until thickened and bubbly; cook and stir for 2 minutes more. Return beef and vegetables to skillet. Heat through, stirring to coat all ingredients with sauce.

7. Serve beef mixture over hot cooked brown rice. Top with orange slices; sprinkle with toasted sesame seeds. Makes 4 servings (¾ cup meat and ½ cup rice each).

Herbed Steak with Balsamic Sauce

The sweet flavor of balsamic vinegar is the star of the sauce.

PER SERVING: 214 cal., 11 g total fat (4 g sat. fat), 74 mg chol., 279 mg sodium, 2 g carb., 0 g fiber, 25 g pro. Exchanges: 3.5 lean meat, 0.5 fat. Carb choices: 0.

1 teaspoon cracked black pepper
2 teaspoons dried Italian seasoning, crushed
1 teaspoon garlic powder
¼ teaspoon salt
2 boneless beef top loin steaks, cut ¾ inch thick
1 tablespoon olive oil
½ cup reduced-sodium beef broth
1 tablespoon balsamic vinegar
1 tablespoon butter
2 tablespoons snipped fresh flat-leaf parsley

1. In a small bowl, combine pepper, Italian seasoning, garlic powder, and salt. Sprinkle evenly over both sides of each steak; rub in with your fingers.

2. In a heavy large skillet, heat oil over medium-low to medium heat. Add steaks; cook until desired doneness, turning once halfway through cooking time. Allow 10 to 13 minutes for medium-rare doneness (145°F) to medium doneness (160°F). Remove steaks from skillet, reserving drippings in skillet. Keep steaks warm.

3. Add broth and vinegar to skillet; stir to scrape up any browned bits from bottom of skillet. Bring to boiling. Boil gently, uncovered, about 4 minutes or until sauce is reduced by half. Remove from heat; stir in butter.

4. Divide sauce among four dinner plates. Cut each steak in half. Place a piece of meat on top of sauce on each plate; sprinkle with parsley. Makes 4 servings.

Ginger Beef Stir-Fry

Add more color by using orange or yellow sweet pepper strips in addition to the red.

PER SERVING: 274 cal., 7 g total fat (1 g sat. fat), 32 mg chol., 552 mg sodium, 34 g carb., 5 g fiber, 20 g pro. Exchanges: 1.5 vegetable, 1.5 starch, 2 very lean meat, 1 fat. Carb choices: 2.

8 ounces beef top round steak
½ cup reduced-sodium beef broth
3 tablespoons reduced-sodium soy sauce
2½ teaspoons cornstarch
2 to 3 teaspoons grated fresh ginger
Nonstick cooking spray
1½ cups sliced fresh mushrooms
1 medium carrot, thinly bias-sliced
3 cups small broccoli florets or 1 pound fresh asparagus spears, trimmed and cut into 2-inch pieces
1 small red sweet pepper, seeded and cut into ¼-inch strips
1 tablespoon cooking oil
2 green onions, bias-sliced into 2-inch pieces
2 cups hot cooked brown rice

1. If desired, partially freeze beef for easier slicing. Trim fat from beef. Thinly slice beef across the grain into bite-size strips; set aside. For sauce, in a small bowl, stir together beef broth, soy sauce, cornstarch, and ginger; set aside.

2. Lightly coat an unheated wok or large nonstick skillet with cooking spray. Preheat over medium-high heat. Add mushrooms and carrot; stir-fry for 2 minutes. Add broccoli and sweet pepper; stir-fry about 2 minutes or until vegetables are crisp-tender. Remove vegetables from wok.

3. Carefully add oil to wok. Add beef; stir-fry for 2 to 3 minutes or until desired doneness. Push beef from center of wok. Stir sauce; add to center of wok. Cook and stir until thickened and bubbly.

4. Return vegetables to wok. Add green onions. Stir ingredients to coat with sauce; heat through. Serve warm over hot cooked brown rice. Makes 4 servings (1 cup beef mixture and ½ cup rice each).

Ginger Beef Stir-Fry

(lighten up!)

Use these strategies for more healthful meals.

1. **Choose** cuts of meat with the words "round" or "loin" in the name (for example, ground round or pork tenderloin), skinless poultry, fish, and dry beans, peas, and lentils.
2. **Buy** fat-free and low-fat milk and yogurt. Taste-test various brands of reduced-fat cheeses to find ones you like.
3. **Stock up** on low-fat snacks such as pretzels, air-popped popcorn, flavored rice cakes, and baked bagel chips.
4. **Choose** soft-style margarines with liquid vegetable oil as the first ingredient. Tub or liquid margarines have less saturated fat than stick margarines.
5. **Try** reduced-fat or fat-free sour cream, cream cheese, mayonnaise, salad dressing, margarine, and tartar sauce.
6. **Select** frozen vegetables that have no butter or sauces.
7. **Look for** reduced-sodium Worcestershire and soy sauces; canned broth, beans, and soups; bouillon cubes; lunch meats; bacon; and ham.
8. **Choose** whole grain breads and crackers to boost fiber.
9. **Bake,** broil, grill, poach, steam, or microwave foods instead of frying.
10. **Sauté** foods in cooking spray, low-sodium broth, or fruit juice.

Bistro Beef Steak with Wild Mushroom Ragoût

Bistro Beef Steak with Wild Mushroom Ragoût

Herbes de Provence is a French blend of eight different dried herbs.

PER SERVING: 206 cal., 8 g total fat (2 g sat. fat), 66 mg chol., 291 mg sodium, 4 g carb., 1 g fiber, 27 g pro. Exchanges: 0.5 vegetable, 3 lean meat, 0.5 fat. Carb choices: 0.

3 cloves garlic, minced
1 teaspoon herbes de Provence
½ teaspoon ground black pepper
¼ teaspoon salt
3 8-ounce boneless beef top loin steaks, cut ¾ inch thick
1 tablespoon olive oil
⅓ cup finely chopped shallots
2 cloves garlic, minced
8 ounces assorted fresh wild mushrooms (oyster, cremini, and/or shiitake), sliced*
¼ cup dry sherry (optional)
1 14-ounce can reduced-sodium beef broth
1 tablespoon cornstarch
1 teaspoon herbes de Provence

1. Preheat broiler. In a small bowl, combine the 3 cloves garlic, the 1 teaspoon herbes de Provence, pepper, and salt. Sprinkle onto steaks; rub in garlic mixture with your fingers.

2. Place steaks on the unheated rack of a broiler pan. Broil 3 to 4 inches from heat for 9 to 11 minutes for medium-rare to medium doneness (145°F to 160°F), turning once.

3. Meanwhile, in a large nonstick skillet, heat oil over medium-high heat. Add shallots and the 2 cloves garlic; cook for 1 to 3 minutes or until shallots are tender. Add mushrooms; cook for 6 to 7 minutes or until mushrooms are tender and any liquid evaporates, stirring occasionally. Remove from heat. If desired, stir in sherry. Return mixture to boiling. Cook for 30 to 60 seconds or until liquid evaporates.

4. In a medium bowl, stir together broth, cornstarch, and the 1 teaspoon herbes de Provence. Stir broth mixture into mushroom mixture in skillet. Cook and stir over medium heat until thickened and bubbly. Cook and stir for 2 minutes more.

5. Cut steaks in half; serve with mushroom ragoût. Makes 6 servings (one 4-ounce steak and ⅓ cup sauce each).

***Test Kitchen Tip:** Remove stems from the oyster and shiitake mushrooms before slicing.

Steak with Chutney Sauce

Chutney is a sweet and spicy condiment used in Indian cooking. Look for mango chutney with other condiments or the foreign foods in the supermarket.

PER SERVING: 269 cal., 8 g total fat (3 g sat. fat), 46 mg chol., 173 mg sodium, 22 g carb., 1 g fiber, 25 g pro. Exchanges: 3.5 lean meat, 0.5 fruit, 1 other carb. Carb choices: 1.5.

1 1½-pound beef flank steak
⅔ cup pineapple juice
⅓ cup mango chutney
1 tablespoon rum or pineapple juice
1 tablespoon rice vinegar
1 clove garlic, minced
¼ teaspoon salt
¼ cup golden raisins
1 teaspoon cornstarch
Mango slices (optional)
Fresh parsley sprigs (optional)

1. Trim fat from steak. Score both sides in a diamond pattern, making shallow diagonal cuts 1 inch apart.

2. For marinade, combine juice, chutney, rum, rice vinegar, garlic, and salt. Place steak in a resealable plastic bag set in a shallow dish. Add marinade; seal bag. Marinate steak in the refrigerator for 2 to 24 hours, turning bag occasionally.

3. Drain steak, reserving marinade. Grill steak on rack of an uncovered grill directly over medium heat for 17 to 21 minutes or until medium doneness (160°F), turning once.

4. Meanwhile, for the sauce, pour reserved marinade into a saucepan; stir in raisins and cornstarch. Cook and stir until thickened and bubbly; cook and stir for 2 minutes more.

5. To serve, thinly slice steak diagonally across the grain. Serve with sauce. If desired, garnish with mango slices and parsley. Makes 6 servings (one 4-ounce steak and scant 1 cup sauce each).

Quick Tip:

Red meat is a great source of iron and zinc, two minerals in short dietary supply for many people. Choose lean cuts of beef, such as flank and tenderloin steaks, lean ground beef, and roasts that are closely trimmed of fat, for the leanest red meats possible.

Dilled Pot Roast

This soul-satisfying dish will remind you of stroganoff with its savory dilled yogurt sauce.

PER SERVING: 313 cal., 8 g total fat (2 g sat. fat), 111 mg chol., 185 mg sodium, 22 g carb., 1 g fiber, 35 g pro. Exchanges: 1.5 starch, 4.5 very lean meat, 1 fat. Carb choices: 1.5.

1 2½- to 3-pound boneless beef chuck pot roast
1 tablespoon cooking oil
½ cup water
1 tablespoon snipped fresh dill or 1 teaspoon dried dill
½ teaspoon ground black pepper
¼ teaspoon salt
½ cup plain low-fat yogurt
2 tablespoons all-purpose flour
4 cups hot cooked noodles

1. If necessary, cut roast to fit into a 3½- or 4-quart slow cooker. In a large skillet, brown roast on all sides in hot oil. Transfer roast to slow cooker; add the water. Sprinkle roast with 2 teaspoons of the fresh dill or ¾ teaspoon of the dried dill, pepper, and salt.

2. Cover and cook on low-heat setting for 10 to 12 hours or on high-heat setting for 5 to 6 hours.

3. Transfer roast to a platter, reserving juices; cover and keep warm. Pour juices into a glass measuring cup; skim off fat. Measure 1 cup reserved juices.

4. For sauce, in a small saucepan, stir together yogurt and flour. Stir in the 1 cup reserved cooking juices and remaining 1 teaspoon fresh dill or ¼ teaspoon dried dill. Cook and stir over medium-low heat until thickened and bubbly. Cook and stir for 1 minute more. Serve sauce with meat and noodles. Makes 8 servings.

Indian Beef Patties with Cucumber Yogurt Sauce

A tangy cucumber sauce complements the patties.

PER SERVING: 241 cal., 12 g total fat (5 g sat. fat), 75 mg chol., 377 mg sodium, 8 g carb., 1 g fiber, 24 g pro. Exchanges: 0.5 milk, 2.5 medium-fat meat, 0.5 vegetable. Carb choices: 0.5.

½ cup finely chopped onion
4 tablespoons finely chopped, seeded fresh jalapeño pepper*
2 tablespoon snipped fresh mint
1 teaspoon ground cumin
2 cloves garlic, minced
½ teaspoon salt
1 pound lean ground beef
4 slices Indian flatbread (optional)
1 recipe Cucumber Yogurt Sauce (see recipe, below)

1. In a medium bowl, combine onion, jalapeño pepper, mint, cumin, garlic, and salt. Add ground meat; mix well. Form into four ¾-inch-thick patties.

2. Grill on rack of an uncovered grill directly over medium heat for 14 to 18 minutes or until done (160°F), turning once. If desired, serve on flatbread. Top with Cucumber Yogurt Sauce. Makes 4 servings.

Cucumber Yogurt Sauce: In a small bowl, combine 1 cup plain low-fat yogurt and ⅔ cup chopped, seeded cucumber. Cover and chill until serving time.

***Test Kitchen Tip:** Because chile peppers contain volatile oils that can burn skin and eyes, avoid direct contact with them. When working with peppers, wear plastic gloves. If you do touch the peppers, wash your hands and nails well.

Indian Beef Patties with Cucumber Yogurt Sauce

(shed the skin)

Leaving the skin on chicken during cooking helps to add flavor and keeps moistness in the meat. The meat doesn't absorb much of the fat from the skin. However, because the skin contains a lot of fat (8 grams of fat with skin versus 3 grams of fat without skin for a 3-ounce portion), removing it before eating chicken significantly lowers the fat and calories (193 calories with skin versus 142 without skin for a 3-ounce portion).

Ginger Chicken with Rice Noodles

This recipe is easily doubled to make four servings.

PER SERVING: 396 cal., 13 g total fat (2 g sat. fat), 82 mg chol., 369 mg sodium, 32 g carb., 3 g fiber, 37 g pro. Exchanges: 2 starch, 4.5 very lean meat, 0.5 vegetable, 1.5 fat. Carb choices: 2.

¼ cup finely chopped green onions
3 teaspoons grated fresh ginger
6 cloves garlic, minced
2 teaspoons olive oil
¼ teaspoon salt
4 skinless, boneless chicken breast halves (about 20 ounces total)
4 ounces dried rice noodles
1 cup chopped carrots
1 teaspoon finely shredded lime peel
2 tablespoons lime juice
4 teaspoons olive oil
2 to 4 tablespoons snipped fresh cilantro
¼ cup coarsely chopped peanuts

1. For rub, in a small bowl, combine green onions, ginger, garlic, the 2 teaspoons oil, and salt. Sprinkle evenly onto chicken; rub in with your fingers.

2. Grill chicken on the rack of an uncovered grill directly over medium heat for 12 to 15 minutes or until tender and no longer pink (170°F), turning once.

3. Meanwhile, in a large saucepan, cook noodles and carrots in a large amount of boiling water for 3 to 4 minutes or just until noodles are tender; drain. Rinse with cold water; drain again. Using kitchen shears, snip noodles into bite-size lengths.

4. In a medium bowl, stir together lime peel, lime juice, and the 4 teaspoons oil. Add noodle mixture and cilantro; toss gently to coat. Divide noodle mixture among four bowls. Thinly slice chicken diagonally; arrange on noodle mixture. Top with peanuts. Makes 4 servings.

Make-Ahead Directions: Rub chicken as directed in Step 1. Cover and chill for up to 24 hours. Prepare as directed in Steps 2 through 4.

Ginger Chicken with Rice Noodles

Penne with Chicken and Broccoli

Penne with Chicken and Broccoli

Light mayonnaise keeps the fat and calories low.

PER SERVING: 309 cal., 9 g total fat (1 g sat. fat), 48 mg chol., 399 mg sodium, 30 g carb., 4 g fiber, 26 g pro. Exchanges: 0.5 vegetable, 2 starch, 2.5 very lean meat, 1 fat. Carb choices: 2.

- **8 ounces dried whole grain penne pasta**
- **3 cups broccoli florets**
- **4 skinless, boneless chicken breast halves (1 to 1¼ pounds total), cut into bite-size pieces**
- **1 teaspoon adobo seasoning**
- **2 tablespoons olive oil, margarine, or butter**
- **1 clove garlic, minced**
- **¼ cup light mayonnaise or salad dressing**
- **⅛ teaspoon ground black pepper**
- **2 tablespoons finely shredded Parmesan cheese**

1. Cook pasta according to package directions, adding broccoli the last 5 minutes; drain. Return to pan.
2. Meanwhile, in a medium bowl, combine chicken and adobo seasoning; toss gently to coat.
3. In a large skillet, heat oil over medium-high heat. Add garlic; cook for 30 seconds. Add chicken; cook for 3 to 4 minutes or until chicken is no longer pink, stirring occasionally.
4. Add chicken to pasta mixture in pan. Stir in mayonnaise and pepper. Cook over low heat until heated through, stirring often.
5. To serve, top pasta mixture with Parmesan. Makes 6 (1⅔-cup) servings.

Jerk Chicken Breasts

The skinless chicken breast halves reduce the fat.

PER SERVING: 180 cal., 3 g total fat (1 g sat. fat), 88 mg chol., 283 mg sodium, 2 g carb., 0 g fiber, 35 g pro. Exchanges: 5 very lean meat. Carb choices: 0.

- **6 skinless, boneless chicken breast halves (about 2 pounds total)**
- **4 teaspoons Jamaican jerk seasoning**
- **8 cloves garlic, minced**
- **2 teaspoons snipped fresh thyme or ½ teaspoon dried thyme, crushed**
- **2 teaspoons finely shredded lemon peel**
- **2 tablespoons lemon juice**
- **Olive oil cooking spray or 2 teaspoons olive oil**
- **Lemon wedges (optional)**

1. Place a chicken breast half between two sheets of plastic wrap; pound gently with the flat side of a meat mallet to an even ½-inch thickness. Repeat with remaining chicken.
2. In a small bowl, combine jerk seasoning, garlic, thyme, and lemon peel. Brush chicken breasts with lemon juice. Sprinkle seasoning mixture evenly onto chicken; rub in with your fingers. Place chicken in a resealable plastic bag; seal bag. Chill in the refrigerator until ready to cook.
3. Coat a cold grill rack with cooking spray. Grill chicken on rack of an uncovered grill directly over medium heat for 6 to 10 minutes or until tender and no longer pink, turning once halfway through grilling. To serve, slice chicken; if desired, serve with lemon wedges. Makes 6 servings.

Broiling Directions: Preheat broiler. Coat the unheated rack of the broiler pan with cooking spray. Place chicken on the rack in the broiler pan. Broil 3 to 4 inches from heat for 6 to 10 minutes or until chicken is tender and no longer pink, turning once halfway through broiling.

Make-Ahead Directions: Prepare chicken as directed through Step 2. Cover and chill for up to 24 hours. Grill or broil as directed.

Jerk Chicken Breasts

Bangkok Stir-Fry

Don't be put off by the aroma of fish sauce. It adds an undetectable yet characteristic flavor to the dish.

PER SERVING: 327 cal., 3 g total fat (1 g sat. fat), 49 mg chol., 541 mg sodium, 49 g carb., 5 g fiber, 26 g protein. Exchanges: 2.5 starch, 0.5 fruit, 2.5 very lean meat, 1 vegetable. Carb choices: 3.

2 tablespoons fish sauce (nam pla)
1 tablespoon lime juice
2 teaspoons minced fresh lemongrass or 1 teaspoon finely shredded lemon peel
Nonstick cooking spray
1 large red onion, cut in thin wedges (1½ cups)
3 cloves garlic, minced
1 small cucumber, cut into thin bite-size strips (1 cup)
¼ of a pineapple, peeled, cored, and cut into ¼-inch wedgess
1 or 2 fresh jalapeño chile peppers, seeded and finely chopped*
12 ounces skinless, boneless chicken breast halves, cut into thin bite-size strips
1 cup sugar snap pea pods, trimmed
2 cups hot cooked brown, jasmine, or basmati rice
Snipped fresh cilantro or parsley (optional)

1. For sauce, in a small bowl, stir together fish sauce, lime juice, and lemongrass; set aside.

2. Coat an unheated large nonstick skillet or wok with cooking spray. Preheat skillet over medium-high heat. Add onion and garlic to hot skillet; cook and stir for 2 minutes. Add cucumber, pineapple, and chile peppers. Cook and stir for 2 minutes more. Remove from skillet.

3. Add chicken to skillet. Cook and stir for 2 to 3 minutes or until chicken is tender and no longer pink. Return onion mixture to skillet; add pea pods. Add sauce. Cook and stir about 1 minute or until heated through. Serve immediately over hot rice. If desired, sprinkle with snipped cilantro. Makes 4 (1-cup) servings.

***Test Kitchen Tip:** Because chile peppers contain volatile oils that can burn your skin and eyes, avoid direct contact with them as much as possible. When working with them, wear plastic or rubber gloves. If your bare hands do touch the peppers, wash your hands and nails well.

Bangkok Stir-Fry

Rosemary Chicken and Artichokes

Chicken with Broccoli and Garlic

Though moist and juicy chicken thighs contain more fat than white meat does, this dish retains its low-cal status. Broccoli slaw and pecans boost the flavor.

PER SERVING: 270 cal., 10 g total fat (2 g sat. fat), 68 mg chol., 392 mg sodium, 24 g carb., 3 g fiber, 23 g pro. Exchanges: 2 vegetable, 1 carb., 2.5 medium-fat meat, 0.5 fat. Carb choices: 1.5.

- **¼ cup all-purpose flour**
- **¼ teaspoon salt**
- **¼ teaspoon ground black pepper**
- **4 medium skinless, boneless chicken thighs (about 12 ounces total), trimmed of fat**
- **1 tablespoon olive oil**
- **6 cloves garlic, minced (about 1 tablspoon)**
- **1 cup reduced-sodium chicken broth**
- **3 tablespoons white wine vinegar**
- **1 tablespoon honey**
- **1 16-ounce package shredded broccoli (broccoli slaw mix)**
- **2 tablespoons coarsely chopped pecans**

1. In a plastic bag, combine flour, salt, and pepper. Add chicken; seal bag. Shake to coat.
2. In a large skillet, cook chicken in hot oil over medium heat for 10 to 12 minutes or until chicken is tender and no longer pink (180°F), turning once. Transfer chicken to plate; cover and keep warm.
3. Add garlic to skillet. Cook and stir for 15 seconds. Add broth, vinegar, and honey. Bring to boiling; reduce heat. Simmer, uncovered, for 5 minutes. Stir in broccoli. Return to boiling; reduce heat. Simmer, covered, for 8 to 10 minutes more or until broccoli is crisp-tender. Stir in pecans. Serve broccoli mixture with chicken. Makes 4 servings (1 thigh and 1 cup broccoli each).

Rosemary Chicken and Artichokes

Start cooking the brown rice first or use microwavable brown rice.

PER SERVING: 168 cal., 4 g total fat (1 g sat. fat), 89 mg chol., 328 mg sodium, 8 g carb., 3 g fiber, 23 g pro. Exchanges: 3 very lean meat, 1.5 vegetable, 0.5 fat. Carb choices: 0.5.

- **1 medium onion, chopped**
- **6 cloves garlic, minced**
- **⅓ cup reduced-sodium chicken broth**
- **1 tablespoon quick-cooking tapioca**
- **2 to 3 teaspoons finely shredded lemon peel**
- **2 teaspoons snipped fresh rosemary or 1 teaspoon dried rosemary, crushed**
- **¾ teaspoon ground black pepper**
- **2½ to 3 pounds chicken thighs, skinned**
- **½ teaspoon salt**
- **1 8- or 9-ounce package frozen artichoke hearts, thawed**
- **1 medium red sweet pepper, cut into strips**
- **Hot cooked brown rice (optional)**
- **Snipped fresh parsley (optional)**
- **Fresh rosemary sprigs (optional)**

1. In a 3½- to 4-quart slow cooker, combine onion, garlic, broth, tapioca, 1 teaspoon of the lemon peel, the snipped rosemary, and ½ teaspoon of the black pepper. Add chicken. Sprinkle with salt and remaining ¼ teaspoon black pepper.
2. Cover and cook on low-heat setting for 5 to 6 hours or on high-heat setting for 2½ to 3 hours.
3. If using low-heat setting, turn cooker to high heat. Add thawed artichokes and pepper strips. Cover; cook for 30 minutes more.
4. To serve, top with remaining 1 to 2 teaspoons lemon peel. If desired, serve with rice, sprinkle with parsley, and garnish with rosemary sprigs. Makes 6 servings.

Feta-Stuffed Chicken Breasts

Even the kids love the feta cheese, tomato, and basil filling.

PER SERVING: 168 cal., 5 g total fat (2 g sat. fat), 75 mg chol., 221 mg sodium, 1 g carb., 0 g fiber, 29 g pro. Exchanges: 4 very lean meat, 2 fat. Carb choices: 0.

1 tablespoon snipped dried tomatoes (not oil-packed)
4 skinless, boneless chicken breast halves (1 to 1½ pounds total)
¼ cup crumbled feta cheese (1 ounce)
2 tablespoons fat-free cream cheese (1 ounce), softened
2 teaspoons snipped fresh basil or ½ teaspoon dried basil, crushed
⅛ teaspoon ground black pepper
1 teaspoon olive oil or cooking oil
Fresh basil sprigs (optional)

1. In a small bowl, pour enough boiling water over the tomatoes to cover. Let stand for 10 minutes. Drain and pat dry; set aside.

2. Using a sharp knife, cut a pocket in each chicken breast by cutting horizontally through the thickest portion to, but not through, the opposite side. Set aside.

3. In a small bowl, combine drained tomatoes, feta cheese, cream cheese, and snipped or dried basil. Spoon about 1 rounded tablespoon into each pocket. If necessary, secure the openings with wooden toothpicks. Sprinkle with pepper.

4. In a large nonstick skillet, cook chicken in hot oil over medium-high heat for 12 to 14 minutes or until tender and no longer pink, turning once (reduce heat if necessary to prevent overbrowning). Serve warm. If desired, garnish with basil sprigs. Makes 4 servings.

Garlic and Mint Chicken Breasts

Garlic and Mint Chicken Breasts

Mint adds a wonderful fresh flavor to this easy dish.

PER SERVING: 202 cal., 6 g total fat (1 g sat. fat), 82 mg chol., 229 mg sodium, 2 g carb., 0 g fiber, 34 g pro. Exchanges: 4.5 very lean meat, 1 fat. Carb choices: 0.

4 skinless, boneless chicken breast halves (1¼ to 1½ pounds total)
½ cup fresh mint
1 tablespoon lemon juice
1 tablespoon olive oil
1 tablespoon reduced-sodium soy sauce
4 cloves garlic
1 teaspoon chili powder
¼ teaspoon ground black pepper
2 cups hot cooked couscous (optional)
Grilled green onions* (optional)
Fresh mint (optional)

1. Place chicken in a resealable plastic bag set in a shallow dish.

2. For marinade, in a blender, combine the ½ cup mint, lemon juice, oil, soy sauce, garlic, chili powder, and pepper. Cover; blend until smooth. Pour over chicken. Seal bag; turn to coat. Marinate in the refrigerator for 4 hours, turning the bag occasionally.

3. Drain chicken, discarding marinade. Grill on rack of an uncovered grill directly over medium heat for 12 to 15 minutes or until tender and no longer pink (170°F), turning once. If desired, serve over couscous with onions; top with mint. Makes 4 servings.

***Test Kitchen Tip:** To grill, place green onions on edge of grill the last 2 minutes of grilling chicken.

Feta-Stuffed Chicken Breasts

(lunches outside of the box)

Do you suffer from S.O.S. Syndrome? You know, the Same Old Sandwich. Packing a lunch gives you control over what you're eating, but it's no fun when lunch is as drab as the brown bag it comes in. Why not get a jump on making lunch interesting by fixing it in advance? Simply prepare and chill Curried Chicken Couscous as directed (see recipe, below) in a microwave-safe container. At lunchtime, just pop the container in the microwave oven to reheat. You'll be the envy of the lunch bunch when you heat up your satisfying meal. Even better, you'll know it's healthful, too.

Curried Chicken Couscous

Curried Chicken Couscous

This recipe is great for those busy nights when your family is on the go and everyone needs to eat at different times. Keep it in your freezer in individual serving bowls.

PER SERVING: 303 cal., 3 g total fat (1 g sat. fat), 59 mg chol., 365 mg sodium, 39 g carb., 3 g fiber, 27 g pro. Exchanges: 0.5 vegetable, 0.5 other carb., 2 starch, 3 very lean meat. Carb choices: 2.5.

Nonstick cooking spray
⅔ cup chopped onion
2 teaspoons curry powder
1 ⅓ cups water
⅔ cup quick-cooking couscous
2 cups cubed cooked chicken breast (about 5 ounces)
⅔ cup loose-pack frozen peas
½ cup fat-free mayonnaise or salad dressing
½ cup chopped red sweet pepper
¼ cup bottled mango chutney

1. Lightly coat four 1½- to 2-cup microwave-safe bowls or mugs with cooking spray. Set aside. Lightly coat an unheated medium skillet with cooking spray.

2. Preheat skillet over medium heat. Add onion; cook and stir until crisp-tender. Stir in curry powder; cook for 1 minute more. Add the water and couscous to skillet; bring to boiling. Remove from heat.

3. Stir in chicken, peas, mayonnaise, sweet pepper, and chutney. Divide among the coated bowls or mugs. Wrap tightly with foil; place in a freezer bag, seal, and freeze for up to 2 months.

4. To serve, remove foil; cover with vented plastic wrap. Microwave on 70 percent power (medium-high) about 3 minutes or until heated through, stirring once. Makes 4 (1¼-cup) servings.

Mediterranean Tostadas

Make the hummus and chicken the day before. The next day, you'll have a great lunch ready to go.

PER SERVING: 413 cal., 7 g total fat (1 g sat. fat), 82 mg chol., 676 mg sodium, 45 g carb., 8 g fiber, 42 g pro. Exchanges: 3 starch, 4 very lean meat. Carb choices: 3.

1 tablespoon olive oil
1 teaspoon lemon juice
¼ teaspoon paprika
Dash salt
Dash freshly ground black pepper
4 medium skinless, boneless chicken breast halves
2 whole wheat pita bread rounds, split and toasted
1 recipe Hummus (see recipe, right)
¾ cup coarsely chopped tomato
½ cup chopped cucumber
Fresh cilantro (optional)
Plain fat-free yogurt (optional)

1. Preheat broiler. In a small bowl, combine oil, lemon juice, paprika, salt, and pepper; set aside.

2. Place chicken on the unheated rack of a broiler pan. Brush both sides of chicken with the oil mixture. Broil 4 to 5 inches from heat for 10 to 12 minutes or until chicken is tender and no longer pink (170°F), turning once. Cool chicken slightly; coarsely chop chicken.

3. To serve, spread Hummus over the toasted pita halves. Top with the chicken, tomato, and cucumber. If desired, garnish with cilantro and serve with yogurt. Makes 4 servings.

Hummus: In a blender or food processor, combine one 15-ounce can garbanzo beans, rinsed and drained; ½ cup chopped fresh cilantro; 3 tablespoons lemon juice or lime juice; 3 tablespoons water; 2 cloves garlic, peeled and halved; ⅛ teaspoon salt; and a dash bottled hot pepper sauce. Cover and blend or process until smooth. Refrigerate until ready to serve. Makes about 1⅓ cups.

Asparagus-Stuffed Turkey Rolls

If you need an impressive entrée in a hurry, this recipe is the answer.

PER SERVING: 142 cal., 2 g fat (1 g sat. fat), 68 mg chol., 271 mg sodium, 3 g carb., 1 g fiber, 28 g pro. Exchanges: 0.5 vegetable, 4 very lean meat. Carb choices: 0.

2 turkey breast tenderloins (about 1 pound total)
16 thin fresh asparagus spears
Nonstick cooking spray
½ cup reduced-sodium chicken broth
2 tablespoons lemon juice
¼ teaspoon salt
⅛ teaspoon ground black pepper

1. Split each turkey breast tenderloin in half horizontally to form a total of 4 turkey steaks. Place each steak between two pieces of plastic wrap. Using the flat side of a meat mallet, lightly pound turkey to ¼-inch thickness. Trim asparagus spears, breaking off woody ends. Arrange 4 asparagus spears on the short end of each turkey piece. Roll up turkey. If necessary, secure with wooden toothpicks.

2. Coat an unheated large nonstick skillet with cooking spray. Preheat skillet over medium heat. Cook turkey rolls in hot skillet until browned, turning to brown evenly. Add broth, lemon juice, salt, and pepper. Bring to boiling; reduce heat. Cover and simmer for 8 to 10 minutes or until turkey is no longer pink.

3. Transfer turkey to serving platter; discard toothpicks. Cover and keep warm. Boil liquid in skillet, uncovered, for 2 to 3 minutes or until reduced to ½ cup. Spoon over turkey. Makes 4 servings.

Quick Tip:

To make meal preparation easier, look for cut-up vegetables in the salad bar of your supermarket. No salad bar? Most supermarkets carry packaged stir-fry vegetables. Use them in salads, casseroles, slow-cooker recipes, and—of course—stir-fries.

Indian-Spiced Turkey Tenderloins

Too cold outside to grill? Use the broiling directions instead.

PER SERVING: 158 cal., 3 g total fat (1 g sat. fat), 73 mg chol., 502 mg sodium, 2 g carb., 1 g fiber, 28 g pro. Exchanges: 4 very lean meat, 0.5 fat. Carb choices: 0.

2 turkey breast tenderloins (about 1 pound total)
1½ teaspoons ground cumin
1½ teaspoons coriander seeds, crushed
1 teaspoon finely shredded lime peel
¾ teaspoon salt
¾ teaspoon ground ginger
¼ to ½ teaspoon crushed red pepper
¼ cup light dairy sour cream
1 tablespoon lime juice

1. Split each turkey tenderloin in half horizontally to form a total of 4 turkey steaks; set aside. In a small bowl, combine cumin, coriander seeds, lime peel, salt, ginger, and crushed red pepper. Set aside ¼ teaspoon of the cumin mixture. Sprinkle remaining cumin mixture over the turkey steaks; rub in with your fingers.

2. Place turkey steaks on the rack of an uncovered grill directly over medium heat. Grill for 12 to 15 minutes or until no longer pink (170°F), turning once halfway through grilling time.

3. Meanwhile, in a small bowl, combine sour cream, lime juice, and reserved cumin mixture. Serve sauce with grilled turkey steaks. Makes 4 servings.

To Broil: Coat the unheated rack of a broiler pan with cooking spray. Place turkey steaks on prepared rack; broil 4 to 5 inches from heat for 8 to 10 minutes or until no longer pink (170°F), turning once halfway through broiling time.

Turkey Tetrazzini

Evaporated fat-free milk gives this Alfredo-style dish just-like-cream flavor without the fat.

PER SERVING: 202 cal., 2 g total fat (1 g sat. fat), 24 mg chol., 253 mg sodium, 32 g carb., 2 g fiber, 17 g pro. Exchanges: 0.5 vegetable, 0.5 milk, 1.5 starch, 1 very lean meat. Carb choices: 2.

4 ounces dried whole wheat spaghetti
2 cups sliced fresh cremini, stemmed shiitake, or button mushrooms
¾ cup chopped red and/or green sweet pepper
½ cup cold water
3 tablespoons all-purpose flour
1 12-ounce can evaporated fat-free milk (1½ cups)
½ teaspoon instant chicken bouillon granules
⅛ teaspoon salt
⅛ teaspoon ground black pepper
Dash ground nutmeg
1 cup chopped cooked turkey breast or chicken breast (about 5 ounces)
¼ cup finely shredded Parmesan cheese (1 ounce)
2 tablespoons snipped fresh parsley
Nonstick cooking spray
Fresh parsley (optional)

1. Preheat oven to 400°F. Cook the spaghetti according to package directions, except omit the cooking oil and only lightly salt the water. Drain well.

2. Meanwhile, in a covered large saucepan, cook the mushrooms and sweet pepper in a small amount of boiling water for 3 to 6 minutes or until the vegetables are tender. Drain well; return to saucepan.

3. In a screw-top jar, combine the ½ cup cold water and flour; cover and shake until well-mixed. Stir flour mixture into the vegetable mixture in saucepan. Stir in evaporated milk, bouillon granules, salt, black pepper, and nutmeg. Cook and stir until thickened and bubbly. Stir in the cooked spaghetti, cooked turkey, Parmesan cheese, and the 2 tablespoons parsley.

4. Lightly coat a 2-quart square baking dish with cooking spray. Spoon spaghetti mixture into dish. Bake, covered, for 10 to 15 minutes or until heated through. If desired, garnish each serving with additional parsley. Makes 6 (about 1-cup) servings.

(turkey talk)

Turkey white meat is naturally low in fat. It has a slightly heartier taste than chicken and is versatile enough to be used as a substitute in place of higher-fat meats. Like all meats, turkey is a good source of iron, zinc, and vitamin B12. If you only think of turkey at holidays, think again—whether you broil it, bake it, or grill it, turkey is a versatile meat for any time of year.

Turkey Tetrazzini

Sage and Cream Turkey Fettucine

Sage and Cream Turkey Fettuccine

Fat-free sour cream adds richness while keeping fat in check.

PER SERVING: 312 cal., 2 g total fat (0 g sat. fat), 60 mg chol., 478 mg sodium, 43 g carb., 2 g fiber, 30 g pro. Exchanges: 2.5 starch, 3 very lean meat, 1 vegetable. Carb choices: 3.

- **6 ounces dried spinach and/or plain fettuccine**
- **⅔ cup fat-free or light dairy sour cream**
- **4 teaspoons all-purpose flour**
- **½ cup reduced-sodium chicken broth**
- **2 teaspoons snipped fresh sage or 1 teaspoon dried sage, crushed**
- **¼ teaspoon ground black pepper**
- **Nonstick cooking spray**
- **12 ounces turkey breast tenderloin steak, cut into bite-size strips**
- **½ teaspoon salt**
- **2 cups sliced fresh mushrooms**
- **4 green onions, sliced**
- **2 cloves garlic, minced**
- **Fresh sage sprigs (optional)**

1. Cook fettuccine according to package directions; drain and set aside.
2. Meanwhile, in a small bowl, stir together sour cream and flour. Gradually stir in broth until smooth. Stir in snipped sage and pepper; set aside.
3. Coat an unheated 8-inch skillet with cooking spray. Preheat over medium-high heat. Sprinkle turkey with salt. Add turkey, mushrooms, green onions, and garlic to hot skillet. Cook and stir about 3 minutes or until turkey is no longer pink.
4. Stir sour cream mixture into turkey mixture. Cook and stir until thickened and bubbly. Cook and stir for 1 minute more.
5. Serve turkey over pasta. If desired, garnish with sage sprigs. Makes 4 servings.

Turkey Scaloppine with Peppers

A squeeze of lime adds a refreshing flavor to this zesty dish.

PER SERVING: 146 cal., 2 g total fat (0 g sat. fat), 51 mg chol., 202 mg sodium, 10 g carb., 1 g fiber, 21 g pro. Exchanges: 0.5 carb., 3 very lean meat. Carb choices: 1.

- **1 12-ounce turkey breast tenderloin**
- **½ cup thinly sliced leek**
- **¼ cup thinly sliced red sweet pepper**
- **1 tablespoon thinly sliced fresh serrano or Anaheim chile pepper***
- **¼ teaspoon salt**
- **⅓ cup all-purpose flour**
- **Nonstick cooking spray**
- **Lime wedges**

1. Cut turkey tenderloin crosswise into 4 pieces; place each piece between two pieces of plastic wrap. Using the flat side of a meat mallet, lightly pound to ¼-inch thickness; remove top piece of plastic wrap. Sprinkle leek, sweet pepper, chile pepper, and salt on both sides of turkey; cover with plastic wrap. Lightly pound to ⅛-inch thickness; remove plastic wrap. Coat with flour, shaking off any excess.
2. Coat an unheated large nonstick skillet with cooking spray. Preheat skillet over medium-high heat. Cook turkey in hot skillet for 6 to 8 minutes or until no longer pink, turning once halfway through cooking time (reduce heat if necessary to prevent overbrowning). Serve with lime wedges. Makes 4 servings.

***Test Kitchen Tip:** Because chile peppers contain oils that can burn your skin and eyes, avoid direct contact with them as much as possible. When working with chile peppers, wear plastic or rubber gloves. If your bare hands do touch the peppers, wash your hands and nails well.

Basil-Buttered Salmon

Use the leftover basil-and-butter mixture to season vegetables.

PER SERVING: 294 cal., 19 g total fat (5 g sat. fat), 94 mg chol., 113 mg sodium, 0 g carb., 0 g fiber, 28 g pro. Exchanges: 4 very lean meat, 1.5 fat. Carb choices: 0.

- **4 fresh or frozen skinless salmon, halibut, or sea bass fillets (about 1¼ pounds total)**
- **½ teaspoon salt-free lemon-pepper seasoning**
- **2 tablespoons butter, softened**
- **1 teaspoon snipped fresh lemon basil, regular basil, or dill or ¼ teaspoon dried basil or dill, crushed**
- **1 teaspoon snipped fresh parsley or cilantro**
- **¼ teaspoon finely shredded lemon peel or lime peel**

1. Thaw fish, if frozen. Rinse fish; pat dry with paper towels. Sprinkle with lemon-pepper seasoning.

2. Place fish on the greased unheated rack of a broiler pan. Turn under any thin portions to make a uniform thickness. Broil 4 inches from heat for 5 minutes. Carefully turn fish. Broil for 3 to 7 minutes more or until fish flakes easily when tested with a fork.

3. Meanwhile, in a small bowl, stir together butter, basil, parsley, and lemon peel. To serve, spoon 1 teaspoon of the butter mixture on top of each fish piece. Cover and chill remaining mixture for another use. Makes 4 servings.

Grilling Directions: Place fish on the greased rack of an uncovered grill directly over medium heat. Grill for 8 to 12 minutes or until fish flakes easily when tested with a fork, carefully turning once halfway through grilling.

Basil-Buttered Salmon

Grilled Sea Bass with Tomatoes

Rub the fish with a garlic and ginger sesame oil mixture before grilling and smother it with a tomato-onion-hot pepper medley.

PER SERVING: 252 cal., 9 g total fat (2 g sat. fat), 69 mg chol., 580 mg sodium, 8 g carb., 2 g fiber, 33 g pro. Exchanges: 1.5 vegetable, 4.5 very lean meat, 1.5 fat. Carb choices: 0.5.

- **4 6-ounce fresh or frozen sea bass or halibut fillets, ¾ to 1 inch thick**
- **4 cloves garlic, minced**
- **1 tablespoon grated fresh ginger**
- **2 teaspoons toasted sesame oil**
- **¾ teaspoon salt**
- **½ teaspoon ground cardamom**
- **4 teaspoons lemon juice**
- **1 medium red onion, sliced ¼ inch thick**
- **1 tablespoon olive oil**
- **2 fresh jalapeño peppers,* seeded and finely chopped (about 3 tablespoons)**
- **3 small yellow or red tomatoes, halved and cut into wedges**
- **1 tablespoon snipped fresh oregano**
- **¾ teaspoon snipped fresh thyme**
- **¼ teaspoon black pepper**

1. Thaw fish, if frozen. Rinse fish; pat dry with paper towels. Set aside.

2. For paste, stir together half of the garlic, the ginger, sesame oil, ½ teaspoon of the salt, and the cardamom. With your fingers, rub both sides of fish evenly with mixture. Cover and chill for 15 minutes. Measure thickness of fish. Grill fish on the greased rack of an uncovered grill directly over medium heat for 4 to 6 minutes per ½-inch thickness or until fish flakes easily when tested with a fork, turning once halfway through grilling time.

3. Meanwhile, in a large heavy skillet, cook onion slices in hot olive oil over medium-high heat until tender, stirring frequently. Add remaining garlic and the jalapeño peppers; continue cooking until onions are golden. Add tomatoes, oregano, thyme, black pepper, and remaining ¼ teaspoon salt. Stir gently until heated through.

4. To serve, place fish on a serving platter; top with the tomato-onion mixture. Makes 4 servings.

***Test Kitchen Tip:** Because chile peppers contain oils that can burn your skin and eyes, avoid direct contact with them as much as possible. When working with chile peppers, wear plastic or rubber gloves. If your bare hands do touch the peppers, wash your hands and nails well.

Grouper with Red Pepper Sauce

Grouper with Red Pepper Sauce

Serve fish on a bed of steamed mixed vegetables.

PER SERVING: 197 cal., 8 g total fat (1 g sat. fat), 42 mg chol., 245 mg sodium, 9 g carb., 2 g dietary fiber, 23 g pro. Exchanges: 1.5 vegetable, 3 very lean meat, 1 fat. Carb choices: 0.5.

- **4 4-ounce fresh or frozen skinless grouper fillets, ½ to 1 inch thick**
- **1 cup chopped red sweet pepper**
- **4 teaspoons butter**
- **2 medium tomatoes, peeled, seeded, and chopped**
- **1 teaspoon sugar**
- **1 teaspoon red wine vinegar**
- **¼ teaspoon salt**
- **⅛ teaspoon garlic powder**
- **Dash cayenne pepper**
- **2 tablespoons lemon juice**
- **4 teaspoons olive oil**
- **¼ teaspoon dried rosemary, crushed**

1. Thaw fish, if frozen; set aside. For sauce, in a small saucepan, cook sweet pepper in hot butter over medium heat until tender. Stir in tomatoes, sugar, vinegar, salt, garlic powder, and cayenne pepper. Cook for 5 minutes more, stirring occasionally. Remove from heat; cool slightly. Transfer mixture to a blender. Cover and blend until smooth. Return to saucepan.

2. Rinse fish; pat dry with paper towels. In a small bowl, combine lemon juice, oil, and rosemary. Brush both sides of fish with lemon mixture.

3. Place fish in a greased wire grill basket, tucking under any thin edges to make a uniform thickness. Place basket on the rack of an uncovered grill directly over medium heat. Grill until fish flakes easily when tested with a fork, turning basket once. (Allow 4 to 6 minutes per ½-inch thickness of fish.)

4. Meanwhile, heat sauce over low heat. Serve the sauce with fish. Makes 4 servings.

To Broil: Place fish on the greased unheated rack of a broiler pan, tucking under any thin edges. Broil about 4 inches from heat. (Allow 4 to 6 minutes per ½-inch thickness of fish.) If fish is 1 inch thick, turn once during broiling.

Curried Seafood with Linguine

Fusion is fun—the pasta may be Italian, but the flavors are Asian.

PER SERVING: 307 cal., 9 g total fat (1 g sat. fat), 42 mg chol., 270 mg sodium, 41 g carb., 3 g fiber, 17 g pro. Exchanges: 2 starch, 1 very lean meat, 1.5 fat, 2 vegetable. Carb choices: 3.

- **4 ounces fresh or frozen medium shrimp in shells**
- **4 ounces fresh or frozen sea scallops**
- **1½ to 2 teaspoons curry powder**
- **6 ounces dried linguine or spaghetti**
- **⅓ cup apricot nectar**
- **1 tablespoon reduced-sodium soy sauce**
- **1 teaspoon cornstarch**
- **¼ teaspoon ground ginger**
- **2 tablespoons cooking oil**
- **1 cup sliced fresh mushrooms**
- **½ cup thinly sliced carrot**
- **3 cups chopped bok choy**
- **2 green onions, bias-sliced into 1-inch pieces**

1. Thaw shrimp and scallops, if frozen. Peel and devein shrimp, leaving tails intact if desired. Halve large scallops. Rinse shrimp and scallops; pat dry with paper towels. In a bowl, toss seafood with curry powder.

2. Cook pasta according to package directions; drain. Cover and keep warm.

3. Meanwhile, in a small bowl, stir together nectar, soy sauce, cornstarch, and ginger; set aside.

4. In a large skillet, heat 1 tablespoon of the oil over medium-high heat. Add mushrooms and carrot; cook and stir for 2 minutes. Add bok choy and green onions; cook and stir for 2 minutes. Remove from skillet.

5. Add remaining 1 tablespoon oil and seafood to skillet. Cook and stir for 2 to 3 minutes or until opaque; push from center. Stir apricot nectar mixture; add to center. Cook and stir until thickened and bubbly. Return vegetables to skillet; stir to coat. Cover and cook for 1 minute.

6. To serve, spoon seafood mixture over hot cooked pasta. Makes 4 servings.

Catfish with Black Bean and Avocado Relish

Another time, try the relish on halibut, orange roughy, or tuna.

PER SERVING: 273 cal., 15 g total fat (3 g sat. fat), 53 mg chol., 337 mg sodium, 14 g carb., 6 g fiber, 23 g pro. Exchanges: 0.5 starch, 3 very lean meat, 0.5 vegetable, 2.5 fat. Carb choices: 0.5.

6 4-ounce fresh or frozen catfish fillets, ½ inch thick
1 teaspoon finely shredded lime peel
3 tablespoons lime juice
2 tablespoons snipped fresh cilantro
2 tablespoons snipped fresh oregano
2 tablespoons finely chopped green onion
1 tablespoon olive oil
¼ teaspoon salt
¼ teaspoon cayenne pepper
1 15-ounce can black beans, rinsed and drained
1 medium avocado, halved, seeded, peeled, and diced
1 medium tomato, chopped
Lime wedges

1. Thaw fish, if frozen. Rinse fish; pat dry with paper towels. Cover and chill until ready to use.
2. For relish, in a small bowl, combine lime peel, lime juice, cilantro, oregano, green onion, oil, salt, and cayenne pepper. In a medium bowl, stir together beans, avocado, and tomato; stir in half of the cilantro mixture. Cover and chill relish until serving time.
3. Grill fish on the greased rack of an uncovered grill directly over medium heat for 4 to 6 minutes or until fish flakes easily when tested with a fork, turning and brushing fish once with the remaining cilantro mixture halfway through grilling.
4. Discard remaining cilantro mixture. Serve fish with relish and lime wedges. Makes 6 servings.

Basil-Lemon Shrimp Linguine

Look for whole grain pasta for more fiber.
Pictured on the cover.

PER SERVING: 336 cal., 6 g total fat (1 g sat. fat), 172 mg chol., 463 mg sodium, 39 g carb., 4 g fiber, 31 g pro. Exchanges: 1 vegetable, 2 starch, 3 very lean meat, 1 fat. Carb choices: 2.5.

1 pound fresh or frozen large shrimp in shells or 12 ounces fresh or frozen sea scallops
6 ounces dried linguini
¼ teaspoon salt
8 ounces fresh asparagus spears, trimmed and cut diagonally into 2-inch pieces
Nonstick cooking spray
2 cloves garlic, minced
1 cup thin yellow, red, and/or green sweet pepper strips
¼ cup snipped fresh basil or 1 tablespoon dried basil, crushed
1 teaspoon finely shredded lemon peel
¼ teaspoon salt
¼ teaspoon ground black pepper
¼ cup sliced green onions
2 tablespoons lemon juice
1 tablespoon olive oil
Lemon wedges (optional))

1. Thaw shrimp, if frozen. Peel shrimp; devein, leaving tails intact if desired. Halve large scallops; rinse well.
2. Cook pasta according to package directions, except use ¼ teaspoon salt and add asparagus the last 3 minutes of cooking; drain.
3. Meanwhile, lightly coat a large nonstick skillet with cooking spray. Heat over medium heat. Add garlic; cook and stir for 15 seconds. Add pepper strips; cook and stir for 2 minutes or until crisp-tender. Add shrimp or scallops (if using), dried basil (if using), lemon peel, ¼ teaspoon salt, and black pepper. Cook and stir for 3 minutes or until shrimp are pink or 3 to 6 minutes or until scallops are opaque. Remove from heat.
4. Add shrimp mixture to pasta mixture. Add snipped fresh basil (if using), green onions, lemon juice, and oil; toss gently to coat. If desired, serve with lemon wedges. Makes 4 (2-cup) servings.

(scallop tips)

There are two basic types of scallops: sea and bay. Bays are smaller and can be tastier, except they're more likely to become overcooked. When purchasing scallops, avoid those that smell fishy or sour, both signs that they aren't fresh. Be aware that a stark bleached-white color or excessive milky liquid in the display tray can be a sign the scallops have been treated heavily with sodium tripolyphosphate (STP). While STP is useful to help bind natural moisture to seafood during the freezing and thawing process, it can be overused and cause scallops to soak up additional water.

Scallops with Anise-Orange Tapenade

Scallops with Anise-Orange Tapenade

The licoricelike flavor of anise and the hint of orange add a bright note to traditional olive relish.

PER SERVING: 145 cal., 3 g total fat (0 g sat. fat), 47 mg chol., 353 mg sodium, 5 g carb., 1 g fiber, 24 g pro. Exchanges: 3.5 very lean meat, 0.5 fat. Carb choices: 0.

- **12 fresh or frozen sea scallops (about 1¼ pounds total)**
- **⅓ cup pitted kalamata olives, coarsely chopped**
- **1 green onion, sliced**
- **½ teaspoon finely shredded orange peel**
- **2 teaspoons orange juice**
- **¼ teaspoon anise seeds, crushed**
- **⅛ teaspoon cayenne pepper**
- **Nonstick cooking spray**
- **Finely shredded orange peel (optional)**

1. Thaw scallops, if frozen. Rinse scallops; pat dry with paper towels. Set aside.
2. For tapenade, in a small bowl, combine olives, green onion, the ½ teaspoon orange peel, orange juice, anise seeds, and cayenne pepper.
3. Coat an unheated large nonstick skillet with cooking spray. Preheat over medium-high heat. Add scallops; cook for 3 to 6 minutes or until scallops are opaque, turning once. Serve warm with tapenade. If desired, top with orange peel. Makes 4 servings.

Szechwan Shrimp

When you see the word "Szechwan," you can expect the dish to pack a little heat.

PER SERVING: 249 cal., 5 g total fat (1 g sat. fat), 129 mg chol., 372 mg sodium, 30 g carb., 0 g fiber, 19 g pro. Exchanges: 2 very lean meat, 2 starch, 0.5 fat. Carb choices: 2.

- **1 pound fresh or frozen medium shrimp in shells**
- **3 tablespoons water**
- **2 tablespoons ketchup**
- **1 tablespoon reduced-sodium soy sauce**
- **1 tablespoon rice wine, dry sherry, or water**
- **2 teaspoons cornstarch**
- **1 teaspoon honey**
- **1 teaspoon grated fresh ginger or ¼ teaspoon ground ginger**
- **½ teaspoon crushed red pepper**
- **½ cup sliced green onions**
- **4 cloves garlic, minced**
- **1 tablespoon peanut oil or cooking oil**
- **2 cups rice noodles or hot cooked rice**
- **2 small fresh red chile peppers (such as Fresno or Thai),* sliced (optional)**

1. Thaw shrimp, if frozen. Peel and devein shrimp. Rinse shrimp; pat dry with paper towels. Set aside.

2. For sauce, in a small bowl, stir together the 3 tablespoons water, ketchup, soy sauce, rice wine, cornstarch, honey, ground ginger (if using), and crushed red pepper. Set aside.

3. In a wok or large skillet, cook and stir green onions, garlic, and fresh ginger (if using) in hot peanut oil over medium-high heat for 30 seconds. Add shrimp. Cook and stir for 2 to 3 minutes or until shrimp are pink; push to side of wok.

4. Stir sauce; add to center of wok. Cook and stir until thickened and bubbly. Cook and stir for 2 minutes more. Serve with rice noodles or rice. If desired, garnish with chile peppers. Makes 4 servings.

***Test Kitchen Tip:** Because chile peppers contain volatile oils that can burn your skin and eyes, avoid direct contact with them as much as possible. When working with chile peppers, wear plastic or rubber gloves. If your bare hands do touch the peppers, wash your hands and nails well.

Szechwan Shrimp

Creole-Style Shrimp and Grits

Creole cooking is a New Orleans specialty that reflects the influences of French, Spanish, and African cuisines.

PER SERVING: 241 cal., 6 g total fat (1 g sat. fat), 129 mg chol., 387 mg sodium, 25 g carb., 2 g fiber, 22 g pro. Exchanges: 1 starch, 2 very lean meat, 2 vegetable, 1 fat. Carb choices: 1.5.

- **1 pound fresh or frozen medium shrimp in shells**
- **½ cup quick-cooking yellow grits**
- **12 ounces fresh asparagus, trimmed and bias-sliced into 2-inch pieces**
- **1 medium red sweet pepper, cut into ½-inch squares**
- **½ cup chopped onion**
- **2 cloves garlic, minced**
- **1 tablespoon olive oil**
- **2 tablespoons all-purpose flour**
- **2 teaspoons salt-free Creole seasoning**
- **¾ cup reduced-sodium chicken broth**
- **¼ teaspoon salt**
- **¼ teaspoon ground black pepper**

1. Thaw shrimp, if frozen. Peel and devein shrimp, leaving tails intact if desired. Rinse shrimp; pat dry. Make grits according to package directions; keep grits warm.

2. Meanwhile, in a large skillet, cook asparagus, sweet pepper, onion, and garlic in hot oil until tender.

3. Stir flour and Creole seasoning into vegetable mixture; add broth all at once. Cook and stir until thickened and bubbly; reduce heat.

4. Stir in shrimp, salt, and black pepper. Cover and cook for 1 to 3 minutes or until shrimp are pink, stirring once. Serve warm over grits. Makes 4 servings.

Garden-Style Ravioli

Convenient purchased ravioli makes cooking dinner a breeze. Vary the vegetables to your own liking.

PER SERVING: 278 cal., 9 g total fat (3 g sat. fat), 26 mg chol., 379 mg sodium, 39 g carb., 2 g fiber, 13 g pro. Exchanges: 2 starch, 0.5 lean meat, 1.5 vegetable, 1 fat. Carb choices: 2.5

- **1 9-ounce package refrigerated light cheese ravioli**
- **1 tablespoon olive oil**
- **2 medium red and/or green sweet peppers, cut into chunks**
- **1 medium carrot, cut into long, thin strips**
- **1 small onion, chopped**
- **2 cloves garlic, minced**
- **1 medium tomato, chopped**
- **¼ cup reduced-sodium chicken broth**
- **1 tablespoon snipped fresh tarragon or 1 teaspoon dried tarragon, crushed, or 3 tablespoons snipped fresh basil or 2 teaspoons dried basil, crushed**
- **Jalapeño pepper (optional)**
- **Fresh tarragon or basil sprig (optional)**

1. Cook ravioli according to package directions, except omit any oil or salt. Drain; return to hot pan.

2. Meanwhile, in a large nonstick skillet, heat oil over medium heat. Add sweet peppers, carrot, onion, and garlic; cook about 5 minutes or until tender. Stir in tomato, broth, and snipped tarragon. Cook and stir about 2 minutes or until heated through.

3. Add sweet pepper mixture to cooked ravioli in pan; toss gently to combine. If desired, garnish with a jalapeño pepper and a tarragon sprig. Makes 4 (1-cup) servings.

Garden-Style Ravioli

Quick Tip:

Lentils, a member of the legume family, are a good source of vegetable protein. Cooked lentils have a beanlike texture and a mild, nutty flavor. For a break from meat, lentils provide a hearty meatless meal. Store lentils, tightly wrapped, in a cool, dry place for up to one year.

Summer Vegetable Pilaf

Summer Vegetable Pilaf

The essences of lemon and fresh basil heighten the flavors of garden-fresh summer vegetables in this lentil-and-rice pilaf.

PER SERVING: 275 cal., 6 g total fat (2 g sat. fat), 8 mg chol., 495 mg sodium, 44 g carb., 11 g fiber, 12 g pro. Exchanges: 1.5 vegetable, 2.5 starch, 1 fat. Carb choices: 3.

1 14½-ounce can vegetable broth
1 medium onion, chopped
½ cup dry lentils, drained and rinsed
½ cup uncooked long grain white rice
¼ cup water
1 teaspoon finely shredded lemon peel
1½ cups small fresh broccoli florets, sliced zucchini or yellow summer squash, and/or fresh snow or sugar snap pea pods
1 medium carrot, cut into thin strips
½ small eggplant, peeled and diced
2 cloves garlic, minced
2 teaspoons olive oil
3 plum tomatoes, chopped
¼ cup snipped fresh basil
¼ cup finely shredded Asiago or Parmesan cheese (1 ounce)

1. In a 3-quart saucepan, combine broth, onion, lentils, uncooked rice, the water, and lemon peel. Bring to boiling; reduce heat. Simmer, covered, for 20 minutes, adding broccoli and carrot during the last 3 to 5 minutes of cooking.

2. Meanwhile, in a 10-inch skillet, cook the eggplant and garlic in hot oil over medium heat until the eggplant is soft, about 5 minutes.

3. Remove lentil mixture from heat; let stand, covered, for 5 minutes. Carefully stir in the eggplant mixture, tomatoes, and basil. To serve, sprinkle with cheese. Makes 4 (1¼-cup) servings.

Mushroom and Asparagus Fettuccine

Rich in protein, earthy mushrooms sub for meat in this colorful pasta dish.

PER SERVING: 319 cal., 8 g total fat (1 g sat. fat), 1 mg chol., 255 mg sodium, 54 g carb., 3 g fiber, 15 g pro. Exchanges: 3 starch, 1.5 vegetable, 1 fat. Carb choices: 3.5.

8 ounces dried whole wheat fettuccine or linguine
8 ounces fresh asparagus, trimmed and cut into 1½-inch pieces
Nonstick cooking spray
3 cups sliced fresh cremini, shiitake, or button mushrooms
1 medium leek, thinly sliced, or ½ cup chopped onion
3 cloves garlic, minced
⅓ cup vegetable broth
¼ cup evaporated fat-free milk
1 tablespoon finely shredded fresh basil or 1 teaspoon dried basil, crushed
1 tablespoon snipped fresh oregano or 1 teaspoon dried oregano, crushed
¼ teaspoon salt
⅛ teaspoon ground black pepper
3 plum tomatoes, chopped
¼ cup pine nuts, toasted
Finely shredded Parmesan cheese (optional)

1. Cook fettuccine or linguine according to package directions, adding asparagus for the last 1 to 2 minutes of the cooking time; drain. Return pasta mixture to saucepan; cover and keep warm.

2. Meanwhile, coat an unheated large nonstick skillet with cooking spray. Preheat over medium-high heat. Add mushrooms, leek, and garlic to hot skillet. Cover and cook for 4 to 5 minutes or until tender, stirring occasionally. Stir in vegetable broth, evaporated milk, dried basil (if using), dried oregano (if using), salt, and pepper. Bring to boiling. Boil gently, uncovered, for 4 to 5 minutes or until mixture is slightly thickened. Stir in tomatoes, fresh basil (if using), and fresh oregano (if using); heat through.

3. Spoon mushroom mixture over pasta mixture; gently toss to coat. Sprinkle with pine nuts and, if desired, Parmesan cheese. Serve immediately. Makes about 4 (1¼-cup) servings.

Pasta with Ricotta and Vegetables

Serve this colorful pasta dish with a simple mixed-greens salad.

PER SERVING: 361 cal., 9 g total fat (2 g sat. fat), 17 mg chol., 408 mg sodium, 55 g carb., 7 g fiber, 16 g pro. Exchanges: 1.5 vegetable, 3 starch, 1 lean meat, 0.5 fat. Carb choices: 4.

- **8 ounces dried cut ziti or penne pasta**
- **2½ cups broccoli florets**
- **1½ cups 1-inch pieces fresh asparagus or green beans**
- **1 cup ricotta cheese**
- **¼ cup snipped fresh basil**
- **1 tablespoon snipped fresh thyme**
- **1 tablespoon balsamic vinegar**
- **1 tablespoon olive oil**
- **1 clove garlic, minced**
- **½ teaspoon salt**
- **½ teaspoon ground black pepper**
- **1⅓ cups chopped, seeded red and/or yellow tomatoes**
- **Shaved Parmesan or Romano cheese (optional)**
- **Fresh thyme sprigs (optional)**

1. Cook pasta according to package directions, adding green beans (if using) with pasta for the whole cooking time or adding broccoli and asparagus (if using) for the last 3 minutes of cooking time. Drain well. Return to hot pan; cover and keep warm.
2. Meanwhile, in a large bowl, combine ricotta cheese, basil, snipped thyme, balsamic vinegar, oil, garlic, salt, and pepper. Gently stir in tomatoes.
3. Add drained pasta mixture to tomato mixture; toss gently to combine. Top with Parmesan cheese. If desired, garnish with thyme sprigs. Makes 4 (2-cup) servings.

Crispy Tofu and Vegetables

The contrast of the crispy, crunchy coating and silken interior of these tofu cutlets may convert the most avowed meat lover.

PER SERVING: 198 cal., 10 g total fat (1 g sat. fat), 0 mg chol., 410 mg sodium, 14 g carb., 3 g fiber, 16 g pro. Exchanges: 1.5 vegetable, 0.5 starch, 1 lean meat, 1 fat. Carb choices: 1.

- **1 10.5-ounce package light extra-firm tofu (fresh bean curd), drained**
- **3 tablespoons reduced-sodium soy sauce**
- **8 green onions**
- **2 cups snow pea pods, strings and tips removed**
- **1 tablespoon toasted sesame oil**
- **1 teaspoon grated fresh ginger or ½ teaspoon ground ginger**
- **1 clove garlic, minced**
- **1 red sweet pepper, seeded and cut into long, thin strips**
- **1 yellow sweet pepper, seeded and cut into long, thin strips**
- **3 tablespoons cornmeal**
- **1 tablespoon white or black sesame seeds, toasted (optional)**

1. Cut tofu crosswise into 8 slices. Arrange slices in one layer on a large plate or jelly-roll pan. Pour soy sauce over tofu; turn slices to coat and let stand for 1 hour.

2. Meanwhile, cut root ends off green onions. Cut off dark green portion of onions, leaving 3 inches of white and light green. Cut green onions in half lengthwise, forming 16 long strips. Set aside. Cut pea pods in half lengthwise. Set aside.

3. Pour oil into a large nonstick skillet. Preheat over medium-high heat. Stir-fry fresh ginger (if using) and garlic for 30 seconds. Add sweet pepper strips and stir-fry for 1 minute. Add green onions and pea pods; stir-fry for 2 to 3 minutes more or until crisp-tender.

4. Drain tofu, reserving soy sauce. Stir reserved soy sauce and, if using, ground ginger into cooked vegetables; transfer vegetable mixture to a serving platter. Cover and keep warm. Carefully dip tofu slices in cornmeal to lightly coat both sides. Cook in same skillet for 3 minutes on each side or until crisp and hot, using a spatula to turn carefully. (You may need to cook tofu slices in two batches; do not crowd skillet.) Serve tofu slices with vegetables. If desired, sprinkle with sesame seeds. Makes 4 servings (2 slices tofu plus 1 cup vegetables each).

Ratatouille over Polenta

Purchased polenta complements this entrée. Look for it in the produce section of your supermarket or with the refrigerated tortillas.

PER SERVING: 260 cal., 8 g total fat (1 g sat. fat), 9 mg chol., 576 mg sodium, 38 g carb., 5 g fiber, 10 g pro. Exchanges: 1 vegetable, 2 starch, 1 fat. Carb choices: 2.5.

- **1 16-ounce tube refrigerated cooked polenta**
- **1 small green sweet pepper, seeded and cut into thin strips**
- **1 small onion, thinly sliced**
- **1 clove garlic, minced**
- **1 tablespoon cooking oil**
- **½ small eggplant, cut into ½-inch pieces**
- **1 large yellow summer squash or zucchini, sliced**
- **1 large tomato, cut into wedges**
- **1 cup small pattypan squash, quartered**
- **1 tablespoon snipped fresh basil**
- **3 tablespoons snipped fresh parsley**
- **Shredded Parmesan cheese (optional)**

1. Cut polenta into 8 to 12 slices and heat according to package directions. Cover and keep warm.

2. For ratatouille, in a 4-quart saucepan, cook the sweet pepper, onion, and garlic in hot oil over medium heat for 5 minutes, stirring frequently. Add the eggplant; cook for 5 minutes more, stirring frequently. Stir in summer squash, tomato, pattypan squash, basil, ⅛ teaspoon *salt*, and ⅛ teaspoon ground *black pepper*. Cook, covered, for 5 to 7 minutes more or until vegetables are tender, stirring occasionally. Stir in parsley.

3. To serve, place 2 slices of polenta each on four to six dinner plates. Spoon warm ratatouille over each serving. If desired, sprinkle with Parmesan cheese. Makes 4 to 6 servings.

Crispy Tofu and Vegetables

main-dish salads

Balsamic Chicken over Greens

Including main-dish salads in your meal plans makes good sense. Pack them with colorful veggies and, to keep the fat and sodium low, make your own dressings or vinaigrettes. A well-crafted salad can be as satisfying as any entrée.

Balsamic Chicken over Greens

Basil adds freshness and flavor to this easy salad.

PER SERVING: 150 cal., 2 g total fat (1 g sat. fat), 66 mg chol., 312 mg sodium, 4 g carb., 1 g fiber, 27 g pro. Exchanges: 1.5 vegetable, 3.5 very lean meat. Carb choices: 0.

4 skinless, boneless chicken breast halves (1 to 1¼ pounds total)
¾ cup bottled fat-free or reduced-fat balsamic vinaigrette salad dressing
3 cloves garlic, minced
¼ teaspoon crushed red pepper
1 8-ounce package torn mixed greens (8 cups)
¼ cup fresh basil leaves

1. Place chicken breast halves in a resealable plastic bag set in a shallow dish.

2. For marinade, combine ½ cup of the vinaigrette, garlic, and pepper; pour onto chicken. Seal bag; turn to coat. Marinate in refrigerator for 1 to 4 hours, turning the bag occasionally.

3. Drain chicken; reserve marinade. Grill on the rack of an uncovered grill directly over medium coals for 12 to 15 minutes or until chicken is no longer pink (170° F), turning and brushing with marinade the last 6 minutes. Discard marinade.

4. Cut each breast across the grain into strips. Arrange greens and basil on four plates; top with chicken strips. Serve with remaining ¼ cup vinaigrette. Makes 4 servings (2 cups greens and 4 ounces chicken each).

Citrus Chicken Salad

Next time you cook chicken breasts, make extra to save for this salad.

PER SERVING: 304 cal., 8 g total fat (2 g sat. fat), 72 mg chol, 422 mg sodium, 28 g carb., 3 g fiber, 31 g pro. Exchanges: 1 vegetable, 0.5 fruit, 0.5 starch, 0.5 other carb., 4 very lean meat, 1 fat. Carb choices: 2.

- **1/4 cup white wine vinegar or cider vinegar**
- **2 tablespoons Dijon-style mustard**
- **1/4 cup snipped fresh oregano or 1 teaspoon dried oregano, crushed**
- **4 teaspoons low-calorie orange marmalade**
- **4 teaspoons salad oil**
- **1/4 teaspoon salt**
- **1/4 teaspoon ground black pepper**
- **4 cups fresh baby spinach**
- **2 11-ounce cans mandarin orange sections, drained**
- **1 cup loose-pack frozen whole kernel corn**
- **12 ounces cooked chicken breast, shredded, or two 6-ounce packages refrigerated cooked chicken breast strips***

1. For dressing, in a screw-top jar, combine vinegar, mustard, oregano, marmalade, oil, salt, and pepper; cover and shake well.

2. In a large bowl, place the spinach, orange sections, and corn. Add dressing and chicken to spinach mixture. Toss to coat. Makes 4 (2-cup) servings.

***Test Kitchen Tip:** If using refrigerated cooked chicken breast strips, omit the 1/8 teaspoon salt from the dressing.

Citrus Chicken Salad

Sesame Chicken Salad

Whole baby corn, colorful radishes, and an aromatic sesame dressing make this a very special salad.

PER SERVING: 154 cal., 5 g total fat (1 g sat. fat), 44 mg chol., 286 mg sodium, 7 g carb., 2 g fiber, 19 g pro. Exchanges: 1.5 vegetable, 2.5 very lean meat, 0.5 fat. Carb choices: 0.5.

- **Nonstick cooking spray**
- **4 skinless, boneless chicken breast halves (1 to 1 1/2 pounds total)**
- **Salt**
- **Ground black pepper**
- **1 10-ounce package torn Italian-style or European-style salad greens**
- **1 14- or 15-ounce can whole baby corn, drained and halved crosswise**
- **1/2 cup coarsely shredded carrot**
- **1/4 cup sliced radishes**
- **1/2 of a large red onion, halved and thinly sliced**
- **1 recipe Sesame-Orange Dressing (see recipe, below)**
- **1 1/2 teaspoons sesame seeds, toasted***

1. Lightly coat an unheated large nonstick skillet with cooking spray. Preheat over medium heat. Sprinkle chicken lightly with salt and pepper. Place in hot skillet. Cook for 10 to 12 minutes or until no longer pink (170°F), turning once halfway through cooking. Transfer chicken to a cutting board. Cut into bite-size strips; set aside to cool slightly.

2. Divide salad greens among six dinner plates. Arrange chicken, whole baby corn, carrot, radishes, and red onion over greens. Pour dressing over salads. Sprinkle with sesame seeds. Makes 6 servings.

Sesame-Orange Dressing: In a screw-top jar, combine 1/2 cup orange juice, 1/4 cup rice vinegar or white vinegar, 1 tablespoon salad oil, 1 teaspoon toasted sesame oil, 1/4 teaspoon salt, and 1/4 teaspoon ground black pepper. Cover and shake well. Chill until serving time.

***Note:** To toast sesame seeds, in a small nonstick skillet, cook and stir sesame seeds over medium heat about 1 minute or just until golden brown. Watch closely so the seeds don't burn. Remove from heat; transfer to a bowl to cool completely.

Grilled Chicken and Wild Rice Salad

Grilled Chicken and Wild Rice Salad

Be sure you're using a plain rice mix instead of one with salty seasonings.

PER SERVING: 262 cal., 2 g total fat (0 g sat. fat), 66 mg chol., 982 mg sodium, 29 g carb., 3 g fiber, 31 g pro. Exchanges: 1 vegetable, 1.5 starch, 3.5 very lean meat. Carb choices: 2.

- **1 6-ounce package long grain and wild rice mix**
- **2/3 cup bottled fat-free Italian salad dressing**
- **6 skinless, boneless chicken breast halves (1 1/2 to 1 3/4 pounds total)**
- **1 cup loose-pack frozen French-cut green beans**
- **1 14-ounce can artichoke hearts, drained and quartered**
- **2 1/2 cups packaged shredded cabbage with carrot (coleslaw mix)**
- **Lettuce leaves (optional)**

1. Prepare long grain and wild rice mix according to package directions. Transfer to a medium bowl. Cover and chill about 2 hours or until cold.
2. Place 3 tablespoons of the Italian salad dressing in a bowl. Set aside remaining dressing.
3. Place chicken on the rack of an uncovered grill directly over medium coals. Grill for 12 to 15 minutes or until chicken is tender and no longer pink (170°F), turning once and brushing with the 3 tablespoons dressing the last 2 minutes.
4. Meanwhile, rinse frozen green beans with cool water for 30 seconds; drain well. In a large bowl, toss together beans, chilled cooked rice mix, artichoke hearts, and coleslaw mix. Pour the reserved Italian salad dressing over the rice mixture; toss gently to coat.
5. Slice grilled chicken; serve over wild rice mixture. If desired, garnish salad with lettuce leaves. Makes 6 servings (1 cup salad and 1 chicken breast half each).

Citrus Turkey Spinach Salad

Pink grapefruit and Orange-Poppy Seed Dressing transform traditional spinach salad into a refreshing meal.

PER SERVING: 251 cal., 10 g total fat (2 g sat. fat), 43 mg chol., 233 mg sodium, 22 g carb., 4 g fiber, 20 g pro. Exchanges: 1 fruit, 2 very lean meat, 1.5 vegetable, 2 fat. Carb choices: 1.5.

8 cups fresh baby spinach or torn fresh spinach
8 ounces cooked turkey, cut up
2 medium pink grapefruit, peeled and sectioned
2 medium oranges, peeled and sectioned
1 recipe Orange-Poppy Seed Dressing (see recipe, right)
2 tablespoons sliced almonds, toasted (optional)

1. In a large bowl, combine spinach, turkey, grapefruit sections, and orange sections.

2. Shake Orange-Poppy Seed Dressing; pour over salad. Toss gently to coat. If desired, sprinkle with almonds. Makes 4 (2-cup) servings.

Orange-Poppy Seed Dressing: In a screw-top jar, combine 1/4 cup orange juice, 2 tablespoons olive oil, 1 teaspoon honey, 1/2 teaspoon poppy seeds, 1/4 teaspoon salt, and 1/4 teaspoon dry mustard. Cover and shake well. Chill until serving time, up to 24 hours.

Citrus Turkey Spinach Salad

Grilled Tuna Salad Niçoise

"Niçoise" means that a food is prepared in the cooking style of Nice, a city in France. Traditional ingredients in salad niçoise include anchovies, potatoes, green beans, ripe olives, and tuna.

PER SERVING: 282 cal., 10 g total fat (1 g sat. fat), 51 mg chol., 408 mg sodium, 17 g carb., 4 g fiber, 31 g pro. Exchanges: 0.5 starch, 3.5 very lean meat, 2 vegetable, 1.5 fat. Carb choices: 1.

1 pound fresh or frozen tuna steaks, cut 1 inch thick
1 recipe Dijon Sherry Vinaigrette (see recipe, below)
8 ounces tiny new potatoes, quartered
6 ounces fresh green beans
6 cups Bibb or Boston lettuce leaves
3/4 cup thinly sliced radishes
1/2 cup niçoise olives or ripe olives, pitted
Finely chopped red onion (optional)
Cracked black pepper (optional)

1. Thaw fish, if frozen. Rinse fish; pat dry with paper towels. Brush fish with 1 tablespoon of the Dijon Sherry Vinaigrette. Set aside remaining vinaigrette.

2. Grill fish on the greased rack of an uncovered grill directly over medium heat for 8 to 12 minutes or until fish flakes easily when tested with a fork, gently turning once halfway through grilling.

3. Meanwhile, in a covered medium saucepan, cook potatoes in boiling water for 7 minutes. Add beans; cook about 2 minutes more or until potatoes are tender. Drain; cool slightly.

4. To serve, slice fish. On a platter, arrange fish, potatoes, beans, lettuce leaves, radish slices, and olives. If desired, top with onion and cracked pepper. Stir remaining vinaigrette; serve with salad. Makes 4 servings.

Broiling Directions: Prepare fish as directed in Step 1. Preheat broiler. Arrange on the greased unheated rack of a broiler pan. Broil about 4 inches from heat for 8 to 12 minutes or until fish flakes easily when tested with a fork, turning once halfway through broiling.

Dijon Sherry Vinaigrette: In a small bowl, combine 3 tablespoons sherry vinegar and 2 tablespoons finely chopped shallots. Whisk in 1 tablespoon Dijon-style mustard. Whisking constantly, pour in 2 tablespoons olive oil in a thin, steady stream. Stir in 1 rinsed and mashed anchovy fillet, 1/8 teaspoon salt, and 1/8 teaspoon ground white pepper. Cover and chill.

Dilled Tuna Potato Salad

Dilled Tuna Potato Salad

Light mayonnaise and fat-free yogurt make a slimmer creamy dressing for this spin on the classic.

PER SERVING: 243 cal., 10 g total fat (2 g sat. fat), 96 mg chol., 461 mg sodium, 22 g carb., 5 g fiber, 18 g pro. Exchanges: 1.5 vegetable, 1 starch, 2 very lean meat, 1.5 fat. Carb choices: 1.5.

3 medium red potatoes (about 1 pound)
1/2 cup light mayonnaise or salad dressing
1/2 cup plain fat-free yogurt
1 tablespoon snipped fresh dill or 1 teaspoon dried dill
1 tablespoon fat-free milk
1/2 teaspoon finely shredded lemon peel
1/4 teaspoon salt
1 clove garlic, minced
1 cup chopped cucumber
1/4 cup sliced green onions
1/4 cup coarsely chopped radishes
1 9-ounce can chunk white tuna (water-pack), drained and broken into chunks
2 hard-cooked eggs, chopped
12 leaves savoy cabbage or Chinese (napa) cabbage

1. Scrub potatoes; cut into 1/2-inch cubes. In a covered medium saucepan, cook potatoes in a small amount of boiling water for 10 to 12 minutes or just until tender. Drain and cool slightly.

2. Meanwhile, in a large bowl, stir together mayonnaise, yogurt, dill, milk, lemon peel, salt, and garlic. Stir in cucumber, green onions, and radishes. Add cooked potatoes, tuna, and eggs; toss gently to coat. Cover and chill for 4 to 6 hours.

3. To serve, line bowls with cabbage leaves. Gently stir tuna mixture; spoon onto cabbage leaves. Makes 6 (1-cup) servings.

(super salads)

Follow a few tips to make your salads the best they can be.

1. Clean and chill ingredients ahead of time. Also chill salad plates and bowls.
2. Add tomatoes to a salad just before tossing to keep them from watering out and diluting the dressing.
3. Mix a tossed salad with its dressing at the last minute to prevent the greens from wilting.
4. Accent salads with red onion or sweet pepper rings, radish roses, pimiento strips, or soynuts.

Salmon and Spinach Salad with Flaxseed Vinaigrette

Salmon and Spinach Salad with Flaxseed Vinaigrette

This hearty bowlful tosses together three health-smart standouts—salmon, spinach, and flaxseeds.

PER SERVING: 239 cal., 15 g total fat (3 g sat. fat), 54 mg chol., 102 mg sodium, 6 g carb., 1 g fiber, 20 g pro. Exchanges: 1 vegetable, 2.5 lean meat, 1.5 fat. Carb choices: 0.5.

12 ounces cooked salmon,* broken into chunks
3 cups fresh baby spinach
1 cup coarsely chopped cucumber
1/2 cup quartered red onion slices
1/4 cup Flaxseed Vinaigrette (see recipe, below)

1. In a large bowl, combine salmon, spinach, cucumber, and red onion. Pour Flaxseed Vinaigrette over salad; toss gently to coat. Makes 4 (1 1/2-cup) servings.

Flaxseed Vinaigrette: Preheat oven to 350°F. In a shallow baking pan, place 1 tablespoon flaxseeds; bake for 10 minutes. Cool. Place toasted flaxseeds in a spice grinder and pulse until ground to a fine powder. In a small bowl, whisk together ground flaxseeds, 3 tablespoons champagne vinegar or white wine vinegar, 2 tablespoons olive oil, 1 tablespoon water, 1 tablespoon finely chopped shallots or green onion, 2 teaspoons Dijon-style mustard, and 1 minced clove garlic. To store, place in a covered container; chill for up to 1 week. Makes about 1/2 cup.

***Test Kitchen Tip:** Cook the salmon by grilling or broiling. You'll need a 1-pound fresh or frozen salmon fillet to get 12 ounces after cooking. Thaw salmon, if frozen. Rinse salmon; pat dry with paper towels.

To Broil Salmon: Preheat broiler. Skin salmon; measure thickness of salmon. Place salmon on the unheated rack of a broiler pan. Broil 4 to 5 inches from heat for 4 to 6 minutes per 1/2-inch thickness of fish or until fish flakes easily when tested with a fork, turning once halfway through broiling.

Salmon Penne Salad with Raspberry Vinaigrette

Brush some vinaigrette onto the salmon, then toss the rest with the pasta salad.

PER SERVING: 368 cal., 14 g total fat (2 g sat. fat), 33 mg chol., 42 mg sodium, 41 g carb., 4 g fiber, 18 g pro. Exchanges: 2.5 starch, 1.5 lean meat, 1 vegetable, 1.5 fat. Carb choices: 3.

1 8- to 10-ounce fresh or frozen skinless, boneless salmon fillet or other fish fillet
1 recipe Raspberry Vinaigrette (see recipe, right)
6 ounces dried penne pasta (about 2 cups)
1 cup bias-sliced fresh asparagus spears
1 cup fresh red raspberries or sliced fresh strawberries
Lettuce leaves (optional)
2 green onions, sliced

1. Thaw fish, if frozen. Rinse fish; pat dry with paper towels. Measure thickness of the fish. Brush fish with 2 teaspoons of the Raspberry Vinaigrette. Cover and chill remaining vinaigrette until ready to use.

2. Preheat broiler. Place fish on the greased unheated rack of broiler pan; tuck under thin edges. Broil 4 inches from heat for 4 to 6 minutes per 1/2-inch thickness of fish or until fish flakes easily when tested with a fork, turning once if 1 inch thick.

3. Meanwhile, cook pasta according to package directions, adding asparagus the last 2 minutes of cooking time. Drain; rinse with cold water. Drain again. Return pasta to pan. Add reserved vinaigrette; toss to coat.

4. Flake cooked salmon. Add salmon to pasta; toss gently. Cover and chill until serving time.

5. To serve, add berries to pasta mixture; toss to mix. If desired, serve on four lettuce-lined plates. Top with green onions. Makes 4 (2-cup) servings.

Raspberry Vinaigrette: In a small bowl, whisk together 1/4 cup raspberry vinegar, 2 tablespoons olive oil, 1 tablespoon honey mustard, 2 teaspoons sugar, 1 minced clove garlic, and 1/4 teaspoon ground black pepper. Cover and chill until serving time.

Make-Ahead Directions: Prepare Raspberry Vinaigrette as directed; cover and chill for up to 24 hours. Make salmon-pasta mixture as directed through Step 4; cover and chill for up to 4 hours. Serve as directed in Step 5.

Crab Cakes with Spring Green Salad

Light mayonnaise and egg white are the low-fat binding for the crab cakes.

PER SERVING: 181 cal., 9 g total fat (1 g sat. fat), 78 mg chol., 426 mg sodium, 8 g carb., 1 g fiber, 18 g pro. Exchanges: 1.5 vegetable, 2 very lean meat, 1.5 fat. Carb choices: 0.5.

- **1 egg white**
- **3 tablespoons light mayonnaise**
- **1 tablespoon Dijon-style mustard**
- **Few drops bottled hot pepper sauce**
- **3 tablespoons finely chopped red or green sweet pepper**
- **2 tablespoons snipped fresh parsley**
- **1 tablespoon sliced green onion**
- **2 teaspoons snipped fresh dill or cilantro or 1/2 teaspoon dried dill weed**
- **1 pound cooked fresh lump crabmeat or three 6- to 6 1/2-ounce cans lump crabmeat, drained, flaked, and cartilage removed**
- **1 1/4 cups soft whole wheat or white bread crumbs**
- **1 recipe Lime Dressing (see recipe, right)**
- **8 ounces mixed baby salad greens (8 cups)**
- **1 head Belgian endive, sliced crosswise**
- **1 medium tomato, seeded and chopped**
- **Nonstick cooking spray**
- **Lime wedges (optional)**

1. In a large bowl, whisk together egg white, mayonnaise, mustard, and hot pepper sauce. Stir in sweet pepper, parsley, green onion, and dill. Add crabmeat and 1/2 cup of the bread crumbs; stir until combined. Using wet hands, shape mixture into six 1/2-inch-thick patties. Place patties in a 15×10×1-inch baking pan. Cover and chill for 30 minutes.

2. Prepare Lime Dressing; set aside. In a large bowl, combine greens, endive, and tomato. Cover and chill until ready to serve.

3. Preheat oven to 300°F. Place remaining 3/4 cup bread crumbs in a shallow dish. Dip crab cakes into bread crumbs, turning to coat both sides. Coat an unheated large nonstick skillet with cooking spray. Preheat over medium heat. Add half of the crab cakes. Cook for 8 to 10 minutes or until golden brown and heated through (160°F), turning once halfway through cooking. Transfer crab cakes to a baking sheet; keep warm in the oven. Repeat with remaining crab cakes.

Quick Tip:

Crab, famous for its sweet, succulent meat, is available in myriad convenient-to-use forms. Look for cooked crabmeat that is frozen, pasteurized (which requires refrigeration), or canned. Claw meat, lump meat, and flaked meat are canned crab options.

4. To serve, toss greens mixture with Lime Dressing; divide among six salad plates. Top with warm crab cakes. If desired, garnish with lime wedges. Makes 6 servings (1 crabcake and 1 1/3 cups salad each).

Lime Dressing: In a small bowl, whisk together 2 tablespoons olive oil, 2 tablespoons lime juice, 1 minced clove garlic, 1/8 teaspoon salt, and 1/8 teaspoon ground black pepper. Cover and chill.

Curried Crab Salad

It only takes 20 minutes to enhance juicy fresh fruit and crabmeat with a light, curry-seasoned dressing.

PER SERVING: 200 cal., 9 g total fat (2 g sat. fat), 58 mg chol., 361 mg sodium, 17 g carb., 2 g fiber, 14 g pro. Exchanges: 1 vegetable, 1 fruit, 0.5 lean meat, 1 fat. Carb choices: 1.

- **4 cups cut-up fresh fruit (such as pineapple, cantaloupe, honeydew melon, and/or strawberries)**
- **2 6-ounce packages frozen crabmeat, thawed**
- **1 1/4 cups sliced celery**
- **1/2 cup light mayonnaise or salad dressing**
- **1/2 cup plain low-fat yogurt**
- **1/4 cup fat-free milk**
- **1 teaspoon curry powder**
- **8 cups torn mixed salad greens**

1. In a very large bowl, for crab salad, combine fresh fruit, crabmeat, and celery; set aside.

2. For dressing, in a small bowl, stir together mayonnaise, yogurt, milk, and curry powder.

3. Divide salad greens among six salad plates. Top with crab salad and dressing. Makes 6 servings (1 1/3 cups greens and about 3/4 cup crab salad each).

(flavor boosters)

Many dishes rely on fat and sodium for flavoring, but there are other ways to get great taste without compromising a well-managed diet. Acidic flavors from citrus and vinegars stimulate the taste buds while adding few, if any, calories and no fat. Herbs pack a concentrated punch into a recipe without adding fat and with very few calories. When using fresh herbs, snip or mince them and toss them in just before serving.

Crab Cakes with Spring Green Salad

Spicy Shrimp Tabbouleh

Spicy Shrimp Tabbouleh

For extra flourish, look for cooked shrimp with tails still on.

PER SERVING: 201 cal., 1 g total fat (0 g sat. fat), 111 mg chol., 495 mg sodium, 32 g carb., 6 g fiber, 16 g pro. Exchanges: 0.5 vegetable, 2 starch, 1.5 very lean meat. Carb choices: 2.

- **1 1/3 cups water**
- **2/3 cup bulgur**
- **1/2 cup bottled fat-free ranch salad dressing**
- **1/2 teaspoon finely shredded lime peel**
- **2 tablespoons lime juice**
- **1/4 teaspoon crushed red pepper**
- **1 cup fresh pea pods, halved crosswise**
- **1/2 cup chopped radishes or daikon**
- **1/2 cup snipped fresh cilantro**
- **1/4 cup bias-sliced green onions**
- **8 ounces peeled and deveined cooked shrimp, halved lengthwise and frozen**

1. In a small saucepan, combine the water and bulgur. Bring to boiling; reduce heat. Cover and simmer about 15 minutes or until most of the water is absorbed and bulgur is tender.

2. Meanwhile, for dressing, in a small bowl, combine ranch dressing, lime peel, lime juice, and red pepper. Cover and chill.

3. Stir pea pods into bulgur; transfer to a large bowl. Stir in radishes, cilantro, green onions, and dressing. Cover and chill for 4 to 24 hours. Stir in shrimp to serve. Makes 4 (1-cup) servings.

Shrimply Delicious Salad

A splash of citrus and a pinch of pepper sauce give shrimp a kick.

PER SERVING: 331 cal., 13 g total fat (1 g sat. fat), 172 mg chol., 192 mg sodium, 30 g carb., 5 g fiber, 27 g pro. Exchanges: 2.5 vegetable, 1 fruit, 3 very lean meat, 2 fat. Carb choices: 2.

PER SERVING WITH SUBSTITUTE: same as above, except 315 cal., 26 g carb. Carb choices: 1.5.

- **1 pound fresh or frozen peeled, deveined large shrimp (leave tails intact, if desired)**
- **1/4 cup orange juice**
- **1/4 cup lime juice**
- **1/2 to 1 teaspoon bottled hot pepper sauce**
- **1/2 teaspoon ground black pepper**
- **8 cups torn mixed salad greens**
- **2 11-ounce cans mandarin orange sections, drained**
- **1 1/2 cups bite-size strips red, green, and/or yellow sweet peppers**
- **1/2 cup thinly sliced red onion**
- **1 recipe Sesame-Citrus Vinaigrette (see recipe, below)**
- **2 tablespoons sesame seeds, toasted**

1. If using wooden skewers, soak in warm water for 30 minutes.
2. Thaw shrimp, if frozen. Rinse shrimp; pat dry with paper towels.
3. In a screw-top jar, combine citrus juices, pepper sauce, and black pepper. Cover and shake to mix.
4. For marinade, place 1/4 cup of the juice mixture in a bowl. Reserve remaining juice mixture to use in Sesame-Citrus Vinaigrette. Add shrimp; toss gently to coat. Cover and marinate in the refrigerator for 1 hour.
5. Drain shrimp, discarding marinade. Thread shrimp onto skewers, leaving a 1/4-inch space between each shrimp.
6. Grill shrimp on the greased rack of an uncovered grill directly over medium coals for 5 to 8 minutes or until shrimp are pink, turning once halfway through grilling.
7. In a large bowl, combine mixed greens, orange sections, sweet peppers, and red onion. Add Sesame-Citrus Vinaigrette; toss gently to coat. Divide among four plates. Arrange shrimp on top of greens. Sprinkle with sesame seeds. Makes 4 (3-cup) servings.

Sesame-Citrus Vinaigrette: To citrus juice mixture in screw-top jar, add 2 tablespoons canola oil, 4 teaspoons sugar or sugar substitute* equivalent to 4 teaspoons sugar, 2 teaspoons red wine vinegar, and 1 teaspoon toasted sesame oil. Cover; shake well. Makes 1 1/3 cups.

Quick Tip:

Shrimp do indeed have cholesterol—about 166 mg in a 3-ounce serving. But they also are low in total fat, saturated fat, and calories. So it's OK to satisfy your craving for shrimp every now and then if you are watching your total cholesterol intake from all of the foods you eat.

Make-Ahead Directions: Prepare as directed through Step 5. Cover and chill shrimp and dressing separately for up to 24 hours. Continue as directed in Step 6.

***Sugar Substitute:** Try Splenda granular. Follow package directions to measure product amount equivalent to 4 teaspoons sugar.

Shrimply Delicious Salad

Grilled Salmon Salad with Oil-Free Vinaigrette

Grilled Salmon Salad with Oil-Free Vinaigrette

Fruit pectin thickens the dressing without fat.

PER SERVING: 228 cal., 9 g total fat (1 g sat. fat), 78 mg chol., 83 mg sodium, 5 g carb., 2 g fiber, 30 g pro. Exchanges: 1.5 vegetable, 4 lean meat. Carb choices: 0.

1 recipe Oil-Free Vinaigrette (see recipe, right)
1 1/4 pounds fresh or frozen salmon fillet
Ground black pepper
Nonstick cooking spray
3 cups torn mixed salad greens
1 cup cucumber slices, halved
1 cup steamed asparagus or green beans, cut into 2-inch pieces and chilled*
1/2 cup radish slices
1/4 cup sliced green onions
Fresh dill sprigs or tarragon sprigs (optional)

1. Prepare Oil-Free Vinaigrette. Thaw salmon, if frozen. Rinse salmon; pat dry with paper towels. Measure thickness of salmon. Cut salmon into four portions. Sprinkle with pepper.

2. Spray an unheated grill rack with cooking spray. Place salmon, skin sides up, on sprayed grill rack directly over medium coals. Grill for 4 to 6 minutes per 1/2-inch thickness of fish or until fish flakes easily when tested with a fork, turning once halfway through grilling. Using a wide metal spatula, lift fillets off skin to a platter. (Scrape skin from rack and discard.)

3. In a large bowl, toss together greens, cucumber, asparagus, radishes, and green onions.

4. To serve, divide greens among plates. Top with salmon. Serve with Oil-Free Vinaigrette. If desired, garnish each serving with fresh dill. Makes 4 servings (1 1/2 cups greens mixture and 1 piece salmon each).

Oil-Free Vinaigrette: In a small bowl, stir together 1 tablespoon powdered fruit pectin, 1 teaspoon snipped fresh dill or tarragon or 1/4 teaspoon crushed dried dill or tarragon, and 1/8 teaspoon ground black pepper. Stir in 1/4 cup water, 2 teaspoons white wine vinegar, and 1 teaspoon honey Dijon-style mustard. Cover; store in the refrigerator for at least 30 minutes or up to 3 days.

***To Steam Vegetables:** Place asparagus or beans in a steamer basket in a saucepan. Add water to just below bottom of basket. Bring water to boiling. Add asparagus or beans to basket. Cover; reduce heat. Steam for 3 to 5 minutes for asparagus or 18 to 22 minutes for beans or until vegetables are crisp-tender.

Broiling Directions: Prepare as directed through Step 1. Preheat broiler. Place salmon, skin sides up, on the unheated rack of broiler pan. Broil 4 to 5 inches from heat for 4 to 6 minutes per 1/2-inch thickness of fish or until fish flakes easily when tested with a fork, turning once halfway through broiling. Continue as directed in Steps 3 and 4.

Grilled Beef and Avocado Salad with Cilantro-Lime Vinaigrette

For the double-duty marinade/salad dressing, jazz up reduced-calorie dressing with zesty lime peel and juice.

PER SERVING: 199 cal., 10 g total fat (3 g sat. fat), 35 mg chol., 477 mg sodium, 8 g carb., 3 g fiber, 20 g pro. Exchanges: 2.5 very lean meat, 1.5 vegetable, 1.5 fat. Carb choices: 0.5.

- **12 ounces beef flank steak**
- **1/2 cup bottled reduced-calorie clear Italian salad dressing**
- **1/2 teaspoon finely shredded lime peel**
- **1/4 cup lime juice**
- **2 tablespoons snipped fresh cilantro**
- **1/4 cup chopped onion**
- **1/4 teaspoon salt**
- **1/4 teaspoon ground black pepper**
- **6 cups torn mixed salad greens**
- **2 small yellow and/or red tomatoes, cut into wedges**
- **1 small avocado, halved, seeded, peeled, and sliced**

1. Score both sides of steak in a diamond pattern by making shallow diagonal cuts at 1-inch intervals. Place in a resealable plastic bag set in a shallow dish.

2. In a screw-top jar, combine salad dressing, lime peel, lime juice, and cilantro. Cover and shake well. Pour half into a small bowl; cover and chill.

3. Add onion to dressing mixture remaining in jar. Cover and shake well; pour over steak in bag. Seal bag; turn to coat steak. Marinate in the refrigerator for 24 hours, turning bag occasionally.

4. Drain beef, discarding marinade. Sprinkle with salt and pepper. Grill steak on rack of an uncovered grill directly over medium heat for 17 to 21 minutes for medium doneness (160°F), turning once.

5. To serve, thinly slice beef across grain. On four plates, arrange greens, tomatoes, beef, and avocado. Add reserved dressing. Makes 4 servings (1 1/4 cups greens and 3 ounces steak each).

Broiling Directions: Prepare steak as directed. Preheat broiler. On unheated rack of broiler pan, broil 3 to 4 inches from heat for 15 to 18 minutes for medium doneness (160°F), turning once. Serve as directed.

Quick Tip:

Making your own dressing isn't as hard as it sounds. Once you do, you'll wonder why you've never made it before. Not only does it taste better than purchased dressings, it is better for you. You control the sodium, sugar, fat, and calories in every bite. Fresh herbs add the finishing touch.

Grilled Summer Vegetable Salad

This side salad is the perfect partner to Balsamic Pork Tenderloin (right), but it goes well with any grilled meat.

PER SERVING: 126 cal., 9 g total fat (1 g sat. fat), 0 mg chol., 55 mg sodium, 11 g carb., 5 g fiber, 2 g pro. Exchanges: 2 vegetable, 1.5 fat. Carb choices: 0.5.

1 medium eggplant, cut crosswise into 1/2-inch slices
1 medium onion, cut into 1/2-inch wedges
2 green and/or red sweet peppers, halved, with stems, membranes, and seeds removed
6 large cremini mushrooms, stems removed
3 roma tomatoes, halved lengthwise
3 tablespoons olive oil
1 tablespoon cider vinegar
1 recipe Herb Vinaigrette (see recipe, right)
Fresh thyme (optional)

1. In a very large bowl, combine eggplant, onion, sweet peppers, mushrooms, and tomatoes. Add oil and vinegar; toss gently to coat.

2. Place vegetables on the rack of an uncovered grill directly over medium-hot coals. (If grilling with Balsamic Pork Tenderloin, arrange vegetables over coals around outside edge of rack.) Grill for 6 to 7 minutes or until tender, turning once.

3. Cut each pepper half into strips. Arrange vegetables on a platter. Drizzle with Herb Vinaigrette. Serve warm or at room temperature. If desired, garnish with thyme. Makes 6 (1-cup) servings.

Herb Vinaigrette: In a small bowl, whisk together 1 tablespoon olive oil, 2 teaspoons cider vinegar, 1 teaspoon snipped fresh parsley, 1/4 teaspoon snipped fresh thyme, 1/4 teaspoon snipped fresh rosemary, 1/8 teaspoon salt, and dash ground black pepper. Makes 2 tablespoons.

Balsamic Pork Tenderloin

To thicken the glaze, simmer or reduce balsamic vinegar to give it more body and flavor.

PER SERVING: 126 cal., 4 g total fat (1 g sat. fat), 49 mg chol., 54 mg sodium, 4 g carb., 0 g fiber, 16 g pro. Exchanges: 2.5 very lean meat, 1 fat. Carb choices: 0.

1 1-pound pork tenderloin
1/4 cup balsamic vinegar
2 tablespoons olive oil
1 tablespoon snipped fresh rosemary
2 cloves garlic, minced
3/4 teaspoon ground black pepper
1/8 teaspoon salt
1 recipe Balsamic Glaze (see recipe, below)
Fresh thyme (optional)

1. Place pork in a large resealable plastic bag set in a shallow dish. For marinade, in a small bowl, whisk together balsamic vinegar, oil, rosemary, garlic, pepper, and salt; pour over meat. Seal bag; turn to coat pork. Marinate in the refrigerator for 1 hour, turning the bag occasionally.

2. Remove pork from marinade, discarding marinade. Prepare grill for indirect grilling. Test for medium heat above the drip pan. Place tenderloin on grill rack over drip pan. Cover and grill tenderloin about 40 minutes or until an instant-read thermometer inserted into the center of the meat registers 155°F.

3. Brush tenderloin on all sides with Balsamic Glaze. Grill for 1 minute more. Remove from grill. Cover with foil; let stand for 15 minutes (the meat's temperature will rise 5°F during standing time). If desired, garnish with fresh thyme. Slice to serve. Serve with Grilled Summer Vegetable Salad (*left*). Makes 6 servings.

Balsamic Glaze: In a small saucepan, bring 1/2 cup balsamic vinegar to boiling. Reduce heat; simmer, uncovered, for 5 minutes. Makes about 1/4 cup.

Balsamic Pork Tenderloin with Grilled Summer Vegetable Salad

(10 great greens)

Becoming familiar with the types of greens available will enable you to enjoy a variety of salads.

1. **Red-tip leaf lettuce** has a tender, sweet, delicate flavor that makes it versatile for many types of green salads.
2. **Leaf lettuce** has a mild, delicate flavor and may be used interchangeably with red-tip leaf lettuce.
3. **Radicchio** is bitter and peppery tasting when eaten alone, but small amounts add a nice accent to other greens.
4. **Spinach** has a mildly hearty flavor and is often used raw in salads.
5. **Swiss chard** has large stems with a delicate flavor similar to celery; leaves have a hearty spinachlike flavor.
6. **Romaine** has large, crisp leaves and a slightly sharp flavor that make this the classic lettuce for Caesar salad.
7. **Curly endive** has a mildly bitter flavor and adds visual interest to salads.
8. **Arugula** has a peppery, pungent flavor that is an ideal contrast when mixed with milder greens.
9. **Mustard greens** have frilly-edge leaves and add a peppery bite to salads, so use torn fresh mustard greens in small amounts.
10. **Dandelion greens** have a slightly bitter flavor with a bite.

(pork perfect)

Pork is a meat you can turn to when you need a meal on the table fast. It's versatile and can be cooked just about any way: grilled, broiled, sautéed, pan broiled, or roasted. Today, the most common cuts of pork produced are 16 percent leaner and have 27 percent less saturated fat than 15 years ago. Also, because of modern feeding practices, trichinosis is no longer a concern. Although trichina is virtually nonexistent in pork today, if it were present, it would be killed at 137°F. That is well below the recommended end cooking temperature for pork, which is 160°F.

Grilled Pork and Pear Salad

Grilled Pork and Pear Salad

Here's a quick dressing trick—stir apple juice concentrate into low-fat mayo and buttermilk.

PER SERVING: 251 cal., 10 g total fat (3 g sat. fat), 50 mg chol., 368 mg sodium, 20 g carb., 4 g fiber, 21 g pro. Exchanges: 1 fruit, 3 very lean meat, 1 vegetable, 1.5 fat. Carb choices: 1.

- **2 boneless pork loin chops (about 12 ounces total), cut 3/4 inch thick**
- **2 teaspoons olive oil**
- **2 teaspoons snipped fresh sage or thyme, or 1 teaspoon dried sage or thyme, crushed**
- **1/4 teaspoon salt**
- **1/4 teaspoon ground black pepper**
- **8 cups torn mixed salad greens**
- **2 medium pears or apples, thinly sliced**
- **1 recipe Creamy Apple Dressing (see recipe, below)**
- **1/4 cup broken walnuts, toasted (optional)**

1. Trim fat from chops; brush chops with oil. In a small bowl, stir together sage, salt, and pepper. Sprinkle sage mixture evenly onto all sides of pork chops; rub in with your fingers.

2. Grill chops on the rack of an uncovered grill directly over medium heat for 9 to 11 minutes or until done (160°F) and juices run clear, turning chops once halfway through grilling.

3. To serve, slice chops. On four plates, arrange greens, pear slices, and pork slices. Stir Creamy Apple Dressing; pour over salad. If desired, sprinkle with walnuts. Makes 4 servings (about 2 cups salad and 3 ounces pork each).

Broiling Directions: Preheat broiler. Prepare chops as directed in Step 1. Arrange on the unheated rack of a broiler pan. Broil 3 to 4 inches from the heat for 9 to 11 minutes or until done (160°F) and juices run clear, turning once. Serve as directed.

Creamy Apple Dressing: In a bowl, stir together 1/2 cup buttermilk; 2 tablespoons low-fat mayonnaise; 1 tablespoon frozen apple juice concentrate or frozen orange juice concentrate, thawed; 1 teaspoon Dijon-style mustard; 1 finely chopped green onion; 1 teaspoon snipped fresh sage or thyme, or 1/4 teaspoon dried sage or thyme, crushed; 1/8 teaspoon salt; and 1/8 teaspoon ground black pepper. Cover and chill until serving time, up to 24 hours.

Roast Pork Salad with Ginger-Pineapple Dressing

Roast Pork Salad with Ginger-Pineapple Dressing

If you use fresh pineapple, cut it up in a bowl and save the juice for the dressing.

PER SERVING: 240 cal., 8 g total fat (2 g sat. fat), 60 mg chol., 219 mg sodium, 22 g carb., 3 g fiber, 19 g pro. Exchanges: 1 fruit, 2.5 very lean meat, 1 vegetable, 1.5 fat. Carb choices: 1.5.

- **12 ounces pork tenderloin**
- **1/8 teaspoon salt**
- **1/8 teaspoon ground black pepper**
- **2 tablespoons honey mustard**
- **6 cups torn romaine and/or fresh spinach**
- **2 cups fresh or canned pineapple chunks and/or sliced fresh nectarines or peaches**
- **Cracked black pepper (optional)**
- **1 recipe Ginger-Pineapple Dressing (see recipe, below)**

1. Preheat oven to 425°F. Trim fat from pork; sprinkle pork with salt and ground black pepper. Place pork on a rack in a shallow roasting pan. Roast for 20 minutes.

2. Spoon mustard onto pork. Roast for 5 to 10 minutes or until an instant-read thermometer inserted in the thickest part registers 160°F.

3. To serve, thinly slice pork. In four salad bowls or plates, arrange greens, pork, and fruit. If desired, sprinkle salads with cracked black pepper. Stir Ginger-Pineapple Dressing; drizzle over salads. Makes 4 servings (1 1/2 cups greens, 3 ounces pork, and 1/2 cup fruit each).

Ginger-Pineapple Dressing: In a small bowl, combine 1/4 cup low-fat mayonnaise, 1/4 cup unsweetened pineapple juice or orange juice, 1 tablespoon honey mustard, and 1 teaspoon grated fresh ginger. Cover; chill until serving time, up to 24 hours.

comforting soups and stews

Vegetable Pasta Soup

Sometimes a bowl of soup is all you need for dinner. These shaped-up, pared-down recipes offer fewer calories but all the flavor to make a meal satisfying. They're perfect when you want something both nourishing and easy.

Vegetable Pasta Soup

Serve this side-dish soup with a sandwich. Or make it a meal of six 1¼-cup servings instead.

PER SERVING: 86 cal., 2 g total fat (1 g sat. fat), 1 mg chol., 227 mg sodium, 14 g carb., 1 g fiber, 4 g pro. Exchanges: 0.5 vegetable, 0.5 starch, 0.5 fat. Carb choices: 1.

2 teaspoons olive oil
6 cloves garlic, minced
1½ cups shredded carrots
1 cup chopped onion
1 cup thinly sliced celery
1 32-ounce box reduced-sodium chicken broth
1½ cups dried ditalini pasta
¼ cup shaved Parmesan cheese (1 ounce)
2 tablespoons snipped fresh parsley

1. In a 5- to 6-quart Dutch oven, heat oil over medium heat. Add garlic; cook and stir for 15 seconds. Add carrots, onion, and celery; cook for 5 to 7 minutes or until tender, stirring occasionally. Add chicken broth and 4 cups *water*; bring to boiling. Add the uncooked pasta; cook for 7 to 8 minutes or until pasta is tender.

2. To serve, top each serving with Parmesan and parsley. Makes 12 (¾-cup) side-dish servings.

Baby Vegetable Minestrone

Baby vegetables are milder in flavor and more tender than their full-size counterparts.

PER SERVING: 77 cal., 2 g total fat (0 g sat. fat), 0 mg chol., 376 mg sodium, 12 g carb., 2 g fiber, 4 g pro. Exchanges: 0.5 starch, 1 vegetable, 0.5 fat. Carb choices: 1.

- **2 teaspoons olive oil**
- **½ cup thinly sliced baby fennel**
- **1 carrot, halved lengthwise and sliced**
- **2 large cloves garlic, minced**
- **¼ teaspoon lemon-pepper seasoning**
- **2 14-ounce cans reduced-sodium chicken broth or 3½ cups homemade chicken broth**
- **½ cup dried ditalini or other small dried pasta**
- **6 ounces baby zucchini, halved lengthwise and sliced**
- **6 ounces baby yellow squash, halved lengthwise and sliced**
- **½ cup sliced green onions**
- **¼ cup fresh basil leaves, thinly sliced**
- **6 ounces Parmigiano-Reggiano or Romano cheese, cut into 6 very thin wedges (optional)**

1. In a very large saucepan, heat oil. Add fennel, carrot, garlic, and lemon pepper; cook and stir over medium heat for 3 to 4 minutes or until carrot is light brown.

2. Carefully stir in broth. Bring to boiling; reduce heat. Simmer, covered, about 8 minutes or until vegetables are just tender.

3. Add pasta. Simmer, covered, for 5 minutes. Add zucchini and squash. Return to boiling; reduce heat. Simmer, covered, for 5 minutes more or until pasta is tender. Stir in green onions and basil.

4. If desired, garnish each serving with a thin wedge of cheese. Makes 6 (1¼-cup) side-dish servings.

Roasted Tomato and Vegetable Soup

For a roasty flavor, buy canned tomatoes that are "fire-roasted."

PER SERVING: 92 cal., 2 g total fat (0 g sat. fat), 0 mg chol., 641 mg sodium, 16 g carb., 4 g fiber, 6 g pro. Exchanges: 0.5 starch, 1 vegetable, 0.5 very lean meat. Carb choices: 1.

- **1 medium onion, chopped**
- **1 stalk celery, sliced**
- **1 medium carrot, chopped**
- **2 cloves garlic, minced**
- **1 tablespoon olive oil**
- **3 14-ounce cans reduced-sodium chicken broth**
- **2 cups cut-up, peeled, and seeded butternut squash**
- **1 14½-ounce can fire-roasted diced tomatoes or diced tomatoes, undrained**
- **1 15- to 19-ounce can white kidney beans (cannellini beans), rinsed and drained**
- **1 small zucchini, halved lengthwise and sliced**
- **1 cup small broccoli and/or cauliflower florets**
- **1 tablespoon snipped fresh oregano or 2 teaspoons dried oregano, crushed**
- **¼ teaspoon salt**
- **¼ teaspoon ground black pepper**
- **Grated Parmesan cheese (optional)**

1. In a 4-quart Dutch oven, cook onion, celery, carrot, and garlic in hot oil over medium heat for 5 minutes or until tender.

2. Stir in chicken broth, squash, and undrained tomatoes. Bring to boiling; reduce heat. Cover and simmer for 20 minutes.

3. Add beans, zucchini, broccoli and/or cauliflower, oregano, salt, and pepper; cook for 5 minutes. If desired, top each serving with grated Parmesan cheese. Makes 8 (about 1⅓-cup) side-dish servings.

Slow-Cooker Directions: Omit the olive oil. In a 3½- to 4-quart slow cooker, combine onion, celery, carrot, garlic, broth, squash, tomatoes, beans, and dried oregano (if using). Cover and cook on low-heat setting for 7 to 8 hours or on high-heat setting for 3½ to 4 hours. If using low-heat setting, turn to high-heat setting. Add zucchini, broccoli and/or cauliflower, fresh oregano (if using), salt, and pepper. Cover; cook about 30 minutes or until tender. Serve as directed.

Quick Tip:

When using a slow cooker for your favorite soup or stew, avoid lifting the lid and peeking into the pot or stirring during cooking. Because the cooker works at low temperatures, the heat that is lost is not easily or quickly recovered and you might need to increase the cooking time.

Roasted Tomato and Vegetable Soup

Dilled Buttermilk-Pea Soup

Whirl tender peas in the blender to thicken this Scandinavian-style soup without flour.

PER SERVING: 83 cal., 1 g total fat (0 g sat. fat), 1 mg chol., 423 mg sodium, 14 g carb., 4 g fiber, 6 g pro. Exchanges: 1 starch. Carb choices: 1.

1 14-ounce can reduced-sodium chicken broth
2 cups shelled fresh peas or one 10-ounce package frozen peas
1 cup torn fresh spinach
¼ cup chopped onion
1 tablespoon snipped fresh dill or savory, or ½ teaspoon dried dill or savory, crushed
¼ teaspoon salt
⅛ teaspoon ground black pepper
½ cup buttermilk
Fresh dill sprigs (optional)

1. In a medium saucepan, combine broth, peas, spinach, onion, snipped herb, salt, and pepper. Bring to boiling; reduce heat. Cover and simmer for 10 to 15 minutes for fresh peas (or 5 to 6 minutes for frozen peas) or until very tender. Cool slightly.

Dilled Buttermilk-Pea Soup

2. In a blender, blend the pea mixture, half at a time, until smooth. Return pureed mixture to same saucepan. Stir in buttermilk.

3. Heat and stir soup until warm. If desired, garnish each serving with fresh dill sprigs. Makes 4 (¾-cup) side-dish servings.

Make-Ahead Directions: Prepare soup as directed through Step 2; cover and chill for up to 24 hours. Serve as directed in Step 3.

Cheddar Cheesehead Soup

Slow and steady cooking keeps the cheese from curdling.

PER SERVING: 147 cal., 5 g total fat (3 g sat. fat), 16 mg chol., 464 mg sodium, 13 g carb., 0 g fiber, 11 g pro. Exchanges: 1 fat-free milk, 0.5 lean meat, 0.5 fat. Carb choices: 1.

1 stalk celery, sliced
1 large onion, coarsely chopped
4 cloves garlic, sliced
1 tablespoon olive oil
3 14-ounce cans reduced-sodium chicken broth
2 12-ounce cans evaporated fat-free milk
½ cup instant flour or all-purpose flour
2 cups shredded reduced-fat cheddar cheese (8 ounces)
¼ teaspoon ground white pepper (optional)
Chopped red sweet pepper (optional)

1. In a Dutch oven, cook celery, onion, and garlic in hot oil until tender. Add chicken broth; bring to boiling. Reduce heat; cover and simmer for 25 minutes.

2. Strain the cooked vegetables, reserving broth in pan. Discard vegetables.

3. Stir together milk and flour; stir into broth. Cook and stir until thickened and bubbly.

4. Add cheese; cook and stir over low heat until cheese is melted. If desired, stir in white pepper; garnish each serving with chopped red sweet pepper. Makes 12 (¾-cup) side-dish servings.

Make-Ahead Directions: Prepare as directed through Step 2. Cover; chill for up to 3 days. Continue as directed in Steps 3 and 4.

(cheese, please)

Many favorite cheeses, such as Monterey Jack, cheddar, mozzarella, American, Swiss, and Parmesan, are readily available in lower-fat versions. But some high-flavor cheeses, such as blue cheese, feta, and Asiago, aren't. However, these cheeses have very pungent flavors and a little goes a long way. Just use them sparingly and you can have your cheese and eat it, too.

Cheddar Cheesehead Soup

Versatile (Asian) Vegetable Soup

Versatile Vegetable Soup

Make three different soups with just one recipe. Choose from two side-dish soups or one main-dish soup.

PER SERVING: 82 cal., 1 g total fat (0 g sat. fat), 0 mg chol., 734 mg sodium, 18 g carb., 4 g fiber, 2 g pro. Exchanges: 0.5 starch, 1.5 vegetable. Carb choices: 1.

- **2 leeks, thinly sliced (white parts only)**
- **3 cloves garlic, minced**
- **1 teaspoon olive oil**
- **8 cups water**
- **1 14½-ounce can stewed tomatoes, undrained**
- **4 stalks celery, sliced**
- **3 medium carrots, thinly sliced**
- **1 medium red apple, cored and coarsely chopped**
- **1 medium sweet potato, peeled and cut into ½-inch cubes**
- **4 teaspoons instant vegetable bouillon granules or vegetable bouillon cubes (to make 4 cups broth)**
- **2 cups shredded cabbage**
- **1 cup cut-up fresh green beans**
- **¼ teaspoon salt**
- **¼ teaspoon ground black pepper**
- **½ cup snipped fresh parsley**
- **2 tablespoons lemon juice**

1. In a 4-quart Dutch oven, cook leeks and garlic in hot oil about 3 minutes or until nearly tender. Carefully add the water, undrained tomatoes, celery, carrots, apple, sweet potato, and bouillon granules. Bring to boiling; reduce heat. Cover and simmer for 15 minutes. Add cabbage, beans, salt, and pepper. Return to boiling; reduce heat. Cover; simmer about 10 minutes or until vegetables are tender. Stir in parsley and lemon juice. Makes 10 (1-cup) side-dish servings.

Asian Vegetable Soup: Prepare as directed, except add ½ cup quick-cooking rice and ½ cup water with the cabbage. Substitute rice vinegar for lemon juice. Add 1 cup thinly sliced fresh mushrooms and 2 thinly sliced green onions with the rice vinegar. Heat through. Makes 10 (about 1¼-cup) side-dish servings.

PER SERVING: 111 cal., 1 g total fat (0 g sat. fat), 0 mg chol., 736 mg sodium, 24 g carb., 4 g fiber, 3 g pro. Exchanges: 1 starch, 1.5 vegetable. Carb choices: 1.5.

Tex-Mex Chicken-Vegetable Soup: Prepare as directed, except cook 1 teaspoon ground cumin with leek. Add 1 cup loose-pack frozen whole kernel corn, 1 cup chopped cooked chicken, one drained 4-ounce can chopped green chile peppers, and 3 tablespoons snipped fresh cilantro with lemon juice; heat through. If desired, garnish each serving with lemon wedges and fresh cilantro. Makes 8 (1⅓-cup) main-dish servings.

PER SERVING: 138 cal., 3 g total fat (1 g sat. fat), 16 mg chol., 790 mg sodium, 23 g carb., 5 g fiber, 8 g pro. Exchanges: 1 starch, 0.5 very lean meat, 1.5 vegetable. Carb choices: 1.

Lemon-Leek Vichyssoise

Low-fat buttermilk brings a pleasant tang to this classic French chilled potato soup.

PER SERVING: 115 cal., 2 g total fat (1 g sat. fat), 2 mg chol., 329 mg sodium, 19 g carb., 1 g fiber, 5 g pro. Exchanges: 1 starch, 0.5 fat. Carb choices: 1.

- **6 medium leeks, trimmed and thinly sliced**
- **2 tablespoons olive oil or cooking oil**
- **3 pounds potatoes, peeled and sliced**
- **3 14-ounce cans reduced-sodium chicken broth**
- **2 teaspoons finely shredded lemon peel**
- **½ teaspoon salt**
- **½ teaspoon ground white pepper**
- **1 quart buttermilk (4 cups)**
- **1 8-ounce carton fat-free or light dairy sour cream**
- **1 tablespoon lemon juice**
- **Lemon wedges (optional)**

1. In a 4- to 5-quart Dutch oven, cook leeks in hot oil until tender. Transfer half to a small container; cover and chill.

2. Add potatoes, broth, lemon peel, salt, and white pepper to leeks in Dutch oven. Bring to boiling; reduce heat. Cover and simmer about 15 minutes or until potatoes are tender. Cool slightly.

3. In a blender or food processor, blend or process potato mixture in small batches until smooth. Transfer to a large container. Stir in buttermilk. Cover and chill until serving time.

4. To serve, ladle soup into small cups or bowls. In a small bowl, combine sour cream and lemon juice; spoon onto soup. Top with chilled leeks. If desired, serve with lemon wedges. Makes 16 (¾-cup) side-dish servings.

Make-Ahead Directions: Prepare soup as directed; cover and chill for up to 48 hours before serving.

Mexican Corn Soup

Serve this chunky, cheesy soup with warm flour tortillas.

PER SERVING: 226 cal., 8 g total fat (4 g sat. fat), 39 mg chol., 471 mg sodium, 23 g carb., 1 g fiber, 17 g pro. Exchanges: 1.5 starch, 1.5 lean meat. Carb choices: 1.5.

1 16-ounce package frozen whole kernel corn, thawed
1 cup reduced-sodium chicken broth
1 4-ounce can diced green chile peppers
1 clove garlic, minced
1 tablespoon snipped fresh oregano or 1 teaspoon dried oregano, crushed
½ teaspoon salt
¼ teaspoon ground black pepper
2 cups fat-free milk
1 cup chopped cooked chicken (about 5 ounces)
1 cup chopped tomatoes
1 cup shredded Monterey Jack cheese (4 ounces)
Snipped fresh parsley (optional)
Fresh oregano sprigs (optional)

1. In a blender, combine half of the corn and the broth; cover and blend until nearly smooth.

2. In a large saucepan, combine corn puree, remaining corn, chile peppers, garlic, dried oregano (if using), salt, and black pepper. Bring to boiling; reduce heat. Simmer, uncovered, for 10 minutes.

3. Stir in milk, cooked chicken, tomatoes, and snipped oregano (if using); heat through. Remove from heat. Add cheese; stir until melted. If desired, garnish each serving with parsley and oregano sprigs. Makes 6 (1-cup) main-dish servings.

Mexican Corn Soup

Quick Tip:

When you're watching your sodium intake, be sure to check the sodium in the broth you use. Here's a comparison of a 1-cup serving of chicken broth:
Low-sodium: 70 mg
Reduced-sodium: 570 mg
Regular: 960 mg
1 bouillon cube: 900 to 1,000 mg

Colorado Lentil Soup

Lentils cook in less time than dry beans and add valuable fiber and no cholesterol.

PER SERVING: 242 cal., 3 g total fat (0 g sat. fat), 0 mg chol., 259 mg sodium, 41 g carb., 16 g fiber, 13 g pro. Exchanges: 1 vegetable, 2.5 starch, 0.5 fat. Carb choices: 3.

1 tablespoon olive oil
1 large onion, chopped
6 cloves garlic, minced
6 cups water
1¼ cups dry brown lentils
1 tablespoon fajita seasoning
1 tablespoon snipped fresh dill or 1½ teaspoons dried dill
¼ teaspoon salt
6 ounces round red potatoes, cut into ¾-inch pieces
1 14½-ounce can no-salt-added diced tomatoes, undrained
1 6-ounce can no-salt-added tomato paste
2 tablespoons canned diced green chile peppers
1 tablespoon snipped fresh parsley
Fat-free dairy sour cream (optional)
Fresh dill sprigs (optional)

1. In a 4-quart Dutch oven, heat olive oil. Add onion and garlic; cook about 4 minutes or until tender.

2. Add the water, dry lentils, fajita seasoning, dried dill (if using), and salt. Bring to boiling; reduce heat. Cover; simmer for 15 minutes. Stir in potatoes. Cook, covered, for 10 to 15 minutes or until tender.

3. Stir in undrained tomatoes, tomato paste, and peppers. Return to boiling; reduce heat. Simmer, uncovered, for 10 minutes.

4. Stir in snipped fresh dill, if using, and parsley. If desired, garnish with sour cream and/or dill sprigs. Makes 6 (1½-cup) main-dish servings.

Sage-White Bean Soup

Sage-White Bean Soup

In the style of country French soups, beans thicken the broth.

PER SERVING: 236 cal., 2 g total fat (0 g sat. fat), 0 mg chol., 630 mg sodium, 40 g carb., 12 g fiber, 15 g pro. Exchanges: 2 starch, 2 very lean meat. Carb choices: 2.

- **1 pound dry Great Northern or navy beans**
- **1 large onion, chopped**
- **1 tablespoon olive oil**
- **12 cloves garlic, minced**
- **4 14-ounce cans reduced-sodium chicken broth**
- **2 tablespoons snipped fresh sage or 2 teaspoons dried sage, crushed**
- **½ teaspoon salt**
- **½ teaspoon ground black pepper**
- **1 recipe Sage French Bread Toasts (see recipe, right) (optional)**
- **Fresh sage leaves (optional)**

1. Rinse beans. In a 4-quart Dutch oven, combine beans and 8 cups water. Bring to boiling; reduce heat. Simmer, uncovered, for 2 minutes. Remove from heat. Cover; let stand for 1 hour. (Or let uncooked beans soak in water overnight.) Drain and rinse beans; set aside.

2. In the same Dutch oven, cook onion in hot oil over medium heat until tender. Add garlic; cook and stir for 1 minute. Stir in beans and broth. Bring to boiling; reduce heat. Cover; simmer for 1 to 1½ hours or until tender.

3. Stir in the snipped or dried sage, salt, and pepper. If desired, top each serving with Sage French Bread Toasts and sage leaves. Makes 8 (1½-cup) main-dish servings.

Sage French Bread Toasts: Preheat oven to 425°F. Brush a little olive oil onto eight ½-inch-thick slices baguette-style French bread. Rub each slice with a cut garlic clove; sprinkle with snipped fresh or crushed dried sage. Bake for 5 to 7 minutes or until light brown.

Chicken Vegetable Soup

Chicken Vegetable Soup

Barley is a tasty addition to this soup. When cooked, pearl barley has a nutty flavor and a slightly chewy texture.

PER SERVING: 249 cal., 5 g total fat (1 g sat. fat), 66 mg chol., 705 mg sodium, 20 g carb., 3 g fiber, 29 g pro. Exchanges: 0.5 vegetable, 1 starch, 3.5 very lean meat, 1 fat. Carb choices: 1.

- **2 pounds skinless, boneless chicken breast halves**
- **1 teaspoon poultry seasoning**
- **2 tablespoons olive oil**
- **1½ cups sliced fresh mushrooms**
- **1 cup chopped carrots**
- **½ cup chopped onion**
- **½ cup chopped green sweet pepper**
- **4 cloves garlic, minced**
- **2 tablespoons snipped fresh basil or 2 teaspoons dried basil, crushed**
- **1 tablespoon snipped fresh parsley or 1 teaspoon dried parsley, crushed**
- **¼ teaspoon ground black pepper**
- **⅛ teaspoon salt**
- **2 tablespoons instant chicken bouillon granules**
- **1 pound potatoes, cut into 1-inch pieces**
- **½ cup quick-cooking barley**

1. Cut chicken into bite-size pieces. In a medium bowl, toss with poultry seasoning; set aside.

2. In a 5- to 6-quart Dutch oven, heat 1 tablespoon of the oil. Add mushrooms, carrots, onion, sweet pepper, garlic, dried basil and parsley (if using), black pepper, and salt; cook for 10 minutes, stirring often. Remove the vegetables.

3. Add remaining 1 tablespoon oil to Dutch oven; heat over medium heat. Add chicken; cook about 5 minutes or until chicken is brown, stirring occasionally.

4. Return vegetables to Dutch oven. Stir in 6 cups *water* and bouillon granules. Bring to boiling; stir in potatoes and barley. Return to boiling; reduce heat. Cover and simmer about 15 minutes or until potatoes are tender. Stir in fresh basil and parsley (if using). Makes 8 (1½-cup) main-dish servings.

Ginger-Chicken Noodle Soup

For a soup that's even quicker, substitute cubed cooked chicken for the chicken thighs and skip the first step.

PER SERVING: 221 cal., 6 g total fat (1 g sat. fat), 72 mg chol., 805 mg sodium, 16 g carb., 2 g fiber, 23 g pro. Exchanges: 1 starch, 3 very lean meat, 1 fat. Carb choices: 1.

- **1 pound skinless, boneless chicken thighs, cut into 1-inch pieces**
- **1 tablespoon cooking oil**
- **2 medium carrots, cut into thin bite-size sticks**
- **3 14-ounce cans reduced-sodium chicken broth**
- **1 cup water**
- **2 tablespoons rice vinegar**
- **1 tablespoon reduced-sodium soy sauce**
- **2 to 3 teaspoons grated fresh ginger or ½ to ¾ teaspoon ground ginger**
- **¼ teaspoon ground black pepper**
- **2 ounces dried rice vermicelli noodles, broken into 2- to 3-inch pieces, or medium noodles**
- **1 6-ounce package frozen pea pods, thawed and halved diagonally**
- **Reduced-sodium soy sauce (optional)**

1. In a Dutch oven, cook chicken, half at a time, in hot oil just until brown. Drain off fat.

2. Return chicken to Dutch oven. Add carrots, broth, the water, vinegar, the 1 tablespoon soy sauce, ginger, and pepper. Bring to boiling; reduce heat. Cover and simmer for 20 minutes.

3. Add noodles. Simmer, uncovered, for 8 to 10 minutes or until noodles are tender, adding pea pods the last 1 to 2 minutes. If desired, serve with additional soy sauce. Makes 5 (1½-cup) main-dish servings.

(lovely leftovers)

When a recipe makes a lot, what do you do? Soups, stews, and casseroles are great served for lunch the next day or frozen for a heat-and-serve meal later in the month. To freeze, divide cooked foods into small portions in shallow containers. As a general rule, divide soups and stews into portions that are two to three inches deep and stir them while cooling to speed the release of heat. Arrange containers in a single layer in the freezer until frozen. Stack them after they are completely frozen. Never let perishable foods stand at room temperature to cool before they're refrigerated or frozen.

Slow-Cooker Chicken Gumbo

Slow-Cooker Chicken Gumbo

Roux ("rue") is generally a mixture of flour and fat that is cooked until very brown and used as a thickener. Here, the flour is browned alone and broth is added to replace the fat.

PER SERVING: 230 cal., 5 g total fat (1 g sat. fat), 48 mg chol., 425 mg sodium, 27 g carb., 3 g fiber, 19 g pro. Exchanges: 0.5 vegetable, 1.5 starch, 2 lean meat. Carb choices: 2.

⅓ cup all-purpose flour
1 14-ounce can reduced-sodium chicken broth
2 cups chopped cooked chicken breast or turkey breast (10 ounces)
8 ounces smoked turkey sausage links, quartered lengthwise and sliced
2 cups sliced fresh okra or one 10-ounce package frozen cut okra, partially thawed
1 cup coarsely chopped onion
1 cup coarsely chopped red or green sweet pepper
½ cup sliced celery
4 cloves garlic, minced
1 teaspoon dried thyme, crushed
½ teaspoon ground black pepper
¼ teaspoon cayenne pepper
3 cups hot cooked brown rice

1. For roux, in a heavy medium saucepan, cook flour over medium heat about 6 minutes or until brown, stirring occasionally. Remove from heat; cool slightly. Gradually stir broth into flour. Cook and stir until thickened and bubbly.

2. Pour roux into a 3½- or 4-quart slow cooker. Add chicken, sausage, okra, 1 cup *water,* onion, sweet pepper, celery, garlic, thyme, black pepper, and cayenne pepper. Cover; cook on low-heat setting for 6 to 7 hours or high-heat setting for 3 to 3½ hours. Skim off fat. Serve over rice. Makes 8 main-dish servings (¾ cup soup and ⅓ cup rice each).

Quick Tip:

Serving soup on a regular basis makes good sense when it comes to eating nutritiously or losing weight. Soups are fairly low in calories and fat (unless it's a cream-base variety) and contain more veggies than meat. And soup fills you up so you'll eat less overall.

Chicken and Rice Soup

What's more comforting than chicken soup? This zesty, Mexican-inspired version.

PER SERVING: 197 cal., 2 g total fat (0 g sat. fat), 33 mg chol., 477 mg sodium, 28 g carb., 2 g fiber, 17 g pro. Exchanges: 0.5 vegetable, 0.5 starch, 2 very lean meat. Carb choices: 2.

- **12 ounces skinless, boneless chicken breast halves**
- **⅓ cup chopped onion**
- **½ teaspoon salt**
- **½ teaspoon ground cumin**
- **½ teaspoon dried oregano, crushed**
- **1 clove garlic, minced**
- **¼ teaspoon ground black pepper**
- **1 bay leaf**
- **1 14-ounce can reduced-sodium beef broth**
- **1 14½-ounce can diced tomatoes, undrained**
- **1 cup frozen whole kernel corn**
- **1 medium green sweet pepper, seeded and chopped**
- **⅔ cup uncooked long grain rice**
- **⅓ cup snipped fresh cilantro**
- **2 teaspoons chili powder**

1. In a Dutch oven, combine 5 cups *water,* chicken, onion, salt, cumin, oregano, garlic, black pepper, and bay leaf. Bring to boiling; reduce heat. Simmer, uncovered, for 10 to 12 minutes or until chicken is no longer pink. Remove chicken and shred into chunks.

2. Stir in broth, undrained tomatoes, corn, sweet pepper, rice, cilantro, and chili powder. Bring to boiling; reduce heat. Simmer, covered, for 25 minutes or until rice is tender. Discard bay leaf. Makes 6 (1⅓-cup) main-dish servings.

Kale, Lentil, and Chicken Soup

Lentils help pack a good amount of fiber into this soothing chicken soup.

PER SERVING: 199 cal., 5 g total fat (1 g sat. fat), 31 mg chol., 833 mg sodium, 20 g carb., 5 g fiber, 18 g pro. Exchanges: 0.5 starch, 2 lean meat, 2.5 vegetable. Carb choices: 1.

- **1 cup chopped onion**
- **1 cup coarsely chopped carrots**
- **2 cloves garlic, minced**
- **1 tablespoon olive oil**
- **6 cups reduced-sodium chicken broth**
- **1 tablespoon snipped fresh basil or 1 teaspoon dried basil, crushed**
- **4 cups coarsely chopped kale (about 8 ounces)**
- **½ teaspoon salt**
- **⅛ teaspoon ground black pepper**
- **1½ cups cubed cooked chicken (about 8 ounces)**
- **1 medium tomato, seeded and chopped**
- **½ cup dry red lentils***

1. In a large saucepan, cover and cook onion, carrots, and garlic in hot oil over medium-low heat for 5 to 7 minutes or until vegetables are nearly tender, stirring occasionally.

2. Add broth and dried basil (if using) to vegetable mixture. Bring to boiling; reduce heat. Cover and simmer for 10 minutes. Stir in kale, salt, and pepper. Return to boiling; reduce heat. Cover and simmer for 10 minutes.

3. Stir in cooked chicken, tomato, red lentils, and fresh basil (if using). Cover and simmer for 5 to 10 minutes or until kale and lentils are tender. Makes 6 (1⅔-cup) main-dish servings.

***Test Kitchen Tip:** If you wish to substitute brown or yellow lentils for the red lentils, you'll need to increase the cooking time. Check the package directions for cooking time and add the lentils in Step 2.

Kale, Lentil, and Chicken Soup

Shrimp and Crab Gumbo

A homemade Cajun spice blend gives this seafood gumbo its classic kick.

PER SERVING: 263 cal., 5 g total fat (1 g sat. fat), 102 mg chol., 510 mg sodium, 31 g carb., 4 g fiber, 22 g pro. Exchanges: 1.5 vegetable, 1.5 starch, 2 very lean meat. Carb choices: 2.

- **1 pound fresh or frozen large shrimp in shells**
- **⅓ cup all-purpose flour**
- **2 tablespoons cooking oil**
- **2 cups chopped onions**
- **1½ cups chopped green and/or red sweet peppers**
- **4 stalks celery, thinly sliced**
- **4 cloves garlic, minced**
- **2 14-ounce cans reduced-sodium beef broth**
- **1 cup water**
- **1 recipe Cajun Spice Mix (see recipe, right)**
- **1 16-ounce package frozen cut okra**
- **2 6-ounce cans crabmeat, drained**
- **3 cups hot cooked long grain rice or brown rice**
- **Green onions (optional)**
- **Bottled hot pepper sauce (optional)**

1. Thaw shrimp, if frozen. Peel and devein shrimp, leaving tails intact if desired. Rinse shrimp; pat dry with paper towels.

2. In a medium skillet, cook flour over medium heat about 6 minutes or until brown, stirring often. Transfer to a medium bowl; set aside.

3. In a 4-quart Dutch oven, heat oil over medium heat. Add onions, sweet peppers, celery, and garlic; cook and stir about 5 minutes or until tender.

Shrimp and Crab Gumbo

4. Slowly whisk broth into browned flour. Add broth mixture, the water, and Cajun Spice Mix to Dutch oven. Stir in okra. Bring to boiling; reduce heat. Cover and simmer for 15 minutes.

5. Add shrimp; cook for 2 to 3 minutes or until shrimp is pink. Gently stir in crabmeat.

6. To serve, spoon gumbo into eight bowls. Top each serving with rice, a shrimp, and, if desired, a green onion. If desired, pass hot pepper sauce. Makes 8 main-dish servings (1¼ cups gumbo and ⅓ cup rice each).

Cajun Spice Mix: In a bowl, combine ½ teaspoon crushed dried thyme, ¼ teaspoon salt, ¼ teaspoon ground white pepper, ¼ teaspoon ground black pepper, and ¼ teaspoon crushed red pepper.

Hot 'n' Spicy Fish Soup

Toast the cumin seeds in a skillet to really bring out the flavor and aroma.

PER SERVING: 252 cal., 9 g total fat (1 g sat. fat), 54 mg chol., 389 mg sodium, 5 g carb., 1 g fiber, 36 g pro. Exchanges: 5 very lean meat, 1 vegetable, 1 fat. Carb choices: 0.

- **4 6-ounce fresh or frozen halibut steaks, cut 1 inch thick**
- **4 teaspoons cooking oil**
- **½ teaspoon cumin seeds**
- **1 medium onion, chopped**
- **3 to 4 teaspoons grated fresh ginger**
- **2 fresh serrano or jalapeño peppers, seeded and finely chopped (see Test Kitchen Tip, page 34)**
- **4 small roma tomatoes, chopped**
- **1 teaspoon ground coriander**
- **½ teaspoon ground turmeric**
- **Fresh cilantro leaves (optional)**

1. Thaw fish, if frozen. Rinse fish; pat dry. Remove skin and bones. Cut into 1-inch pieces; set aside.

2. In a medium saucepan, heat oil over medium heat. Add cumin seeds; cook and stir about 1 minute or until toasted. Add onion; cook and stir for 4 to 5 minutes or until tender. Add ginger and peppers; cook and stir for 1 minute. Add tomatoes; cook and stir for 2 to 3 minutes or until soft. Stir in 1½ cups *water,* coriander, turmeric, and ½ teaspoon *salt.* Bring just to boiling; reduce heat. Stir in fish.

3. Cover and cook about 5 minutes or just until fish flakes easily when tested with a fork. If desired, garnish with cilantro. Makes 4 (1-cup) main-dish servings.

Creamy Seafood Soup with Basil

Fat-free half-and-half steps in for the usual cream.

PER SERVING: 79 cal., 4 g total fat (1 g sat. fat), 16 mg chol., 456 mg sodium, 7 g carb., 0 g fiber, 3 g pro. Exchanges: 0.5 carb., 0.5 very lean meat, 0.5 fat. Carb choices: 0.5.

- **2 pounds live mussels in shells or 12 ounces small shrimp in shells***
- **12 quarts cold water (48 cups)**
- **1 cup salt**
- **1 14-ounce can reduced-sodium chicken broth**
- **1 tablespoon olive oil**
- **1 cup finely chopped leeks****
- **2 cloves garlic, minced**
- **¼ teaspoon saffron threads or ⅛ teaspoon ground turmeric**
- **¼ teaspoon ground black pepper**
- **1 cup fat-free half-and-half**
- **1 tablespoon finely shredded fresh basil**

1. Scrub live mussels under cold running water. Using a sharp knife, cut off the beards between the shells. In a very large bowl, combine 4 quarts (16 cups) of the cold water and ⅓ cup of the salt. Add mussels; soak for 15 minutes. Drain in a colander. Rinse mussels, discarding water. Repeat twice, using fresh salted water. Rinse well. (If using shrimp, omit this step.)

2. In a Dutch oven, combine broth and 1½ cups *water;* bring to boiling. Add mussels; reduce heat. Cover and simmer for 5 to 7 minutes or until shells open. Discard any that do not open. (If using shrimp, cover and simmer in broth mixture for 2 to 3 minutes or until pink.)

3. Strain cooking liquid through a cheesecloth-lined sieve into a large bowl; set aside. Set aside mussels or shrimp until cool enough to handle.

4. In a large saucepan, heat oil over medium heat. Add leeks and garlic; cook and stir for 3 to 5 minutes or until tender. Stir in reserved cooking liquid, saffron, and pepper. Bring to boiling; reduce heat. Simmer gently, uncovered, about 15 minutes or until liquid is reduced to 3 cups total. Stir in half-and-half; heat through.

5. Meanwhile, when mussels are cool enough to handle, remove meat from mussel shells and set aside; discard shells. (Or peel and devein the shrimp; discard shells.)

6. Just before serving, stir the mussels or shrimp into soup; heat through. Sprinkle each serving with basil. Makes 8 (⅔-cup) side-dish servings.

***Test Kitchen Tip:** If using shrimp, add ⅛ teaspoon salt to soup. Omit the 12 quarts water and 1 cup salt.

****Test Kitchen Tip:** To clean leeks, remove root ends and any heavy dark green portions. Slice lengthwise and submerge in a bowl of cool, clean water. Gently open layers and rinse thoroughly to remove any grit or sand. Repeat washing as needed.

sensational sandwiches

Spinach Panini

Sandwiches make great meals when you're in a hurry. From classics to panini to burgers, our ideas offer a range of flavors and fillers designed for you. Or think outside the usual bread and choose from our wraps, pockets, and roll-ups.

Spinach Panini

Spinach boosts the nutrition while basil and feta cheese push the flavor over the top.

PER PANINI: 189 cal., 6 g total fat (3 g sat. fat), 17 mg chol., 471 mg sodium, 25 g carb., 5 g fiber, 10 g pro. Exchanges: 1.5 vegetable, 1.5 starch, 0.5 medium-fat meat. Carb choices: 1.5.

Nonstick olive oil cooking spray
8 slices whole wheat bread or 2 whole wheat pita bread rounds, halved crosswise and split horizontally
4 cups fresh baby spinach leaves
8 thin tomato slices (1 medium tomato)
⅛ teaspoon freshly ground black pepper
¼ cup thinly sliced red onion
2 tablespoons shredded fresh basil leaves
½ cup crumbled feta cheese (1 ounce)

1. Lightly coat an unheated panini griddle, covered indoor electric grill, or large nonstick skillet with cooking spray; set aside.
2. Place 4 of the bread slices or 4 pita pieces on a work surface; divide half of the spinach leaves among bread slices or pita pieces. Top spinach with tomato slices. Sprinkle with pepper. Add onion and basil. Top with feta and remaining spinach. Top with bread slices or pita pieces. Press down firmly.
3. Preheat griddle, grill, or skillet over medium heat or heat according to manufacturer's directions. Add sandwiches, in batches if necessary. If using griddle or grill, close lid and grill for 2 to 3 minutes or until bread is toasted. (If using skillet, place a heavy plate on top of sandwiches. Cook for 1 to 2 minutes or until bottoms are toasted. Carefully remove plate, which may be hot. Turn sandwiches and top with the plate. Cook for 1 to 2 minutes more or until bread is toasted.) Makes 4 panini.

Avocado and Cream Cheese on Bagels

Here is a sandwich to count on for a quick at-home or assemble-at-work meatless lunch.

PER SERVING: 222 cal., 8 g total fat (3 g sat. fat), 13 mg chol., 301 mg sodium, 31 g carb., 5 g fiber, 9 g pro. Exchanges: 1 vegetable, 1.5 starch, 1.5 fat. Carb choices: 2.

½ of an 8-ounce tub light cream cheese
1 tablespoon snipped fresh dill or 1 teaspoon dried dill
¼ teaspoon salt
⅛ teaspoon ground black pepper
4 whole wheat bagel halves, toasted
½ of a medium cucumber, sliced
½ of a medium onion, sliced
½ of a medium avocado, halved, seeded, peeled, and sliced
¾ cup bottled roasted red sweet peppers, drained and cut into thin strips
Fresh dill sprigs (optional)

1. In a bowl, combine cream cheese, snipped or dried dill, salt, and black pepper. Spread onto bagel halves. Top with cucumber slices, onion slices, avocado slices, and red pepper strips. If desired, garnish with fresh dill sprigs. Makes 4 servings.

Veggie Salad in a Pocket

Enjoy leftover Spicy Hummus as a snack with vegetable dippers. Two tablespoons of dip contains 50 calories and 9 grams of carbs.

PER SERVING: 166 cal., 2 g total fat (0 g sat. fat), 0 mg chol., 599 mg sodium, 31 g carb., 6 g fiber, 7 g pro. Exchanges: 0.5 carb. Carb choices: 1.5.

1 cup chopped yellow summer squash and/or zucchini
¾ cup chopped broccoli
2 roma tomatoes, seeded and chopped
8 pitted kalamata or ripe olives, chopped
2 tablespoons snipped fresh flat-leaf or regular parsley
2 tablespoons bottled fat-free Italian salad dressing
2 6- to 7-inch whole wheat pita bread rounds, halved crosswise, or four 6- to 7-inch whole wheat flour tortillas
½ cup Spicy Hummus (see recipe, below)

1. In a medium bowl, combine squash, broccoli, tomatoes, olives, and parsley; toss with salad dressing.

2. Spread insides of pita halves or tortillas each with 2 tablespoons Spicy Hummus.

3. For each sandwich, fill pita half with squash mixture or spoon onto tortilla. Fold or roll tortilla, if using. Makes 4 servings.

Spicy Hummus: In a food processor, combine one 15- to 19-ounce can navy or cannellini beans (white kidney beans), rinsed and drained; ¼ cup bottled fat-free Italian salad dressing; and 1 tablespoon spicy brown mustard. Cover and process until smooth and spreadable. (Or use a potato masher or fork to mash beans. Stir in salad dressing and mustard.) To store, transfer to an airtight storage container. Cover and chill for up to 1 week. Makes 1⅓ cups.

(super sandwiches)

A sandwich can be a humble lunch or a spectacular meal; it's all in how you make it. When you get creative and take advantage of the infinite combinations, a sandwich is something to look forward to. Pita bread, wraps, and breads of all types can take a simple sandwich filling to new heights. But when you experiment with the fillings, the possibilities are endless! A new sandwich to look forward to (like Veggie Salad in a Pocket) can jolt you out of your monotonous noontime rut.

Veggie Salad in a Pocket

Salad Niçoise on Flatbread

Tuna Salad Pockets

Tuna Salad Pockets

Keep the vinaigrette in the fridge for last-minute sandwiches.

PER SERVING: 272 cal., 10 g total fat (2 g sat. fat), 36 mg chol., 659 mg sodium, 22 g carb., 3 g fiber, 25 g pro. Exchanges: 2 vegetable, 1 starch, 2.5 very lean meat, 2 fat. Carb choices: 1.5.

- **1 12-ounce can solid white tuna (water-pack), drained and broken into chunks**
- **¼ cup finely chopped onion**
- **¼ cup thinly sliced celery**
- **¼ cup shredded carrot**
- **1 tablespoon capers, rinsed and drained**
- **1 recipe Dijon Vinaigrette (see recipe, right)**
- **1½ cups torn mixed salad greens**
- **2 large whole wheat pita bread rounds, halved crosswise**

1. In a medium bowl, combine tuna, onion, celery, carrot, and capers.

2. Pour Dijon Vinaigrette over tuna mixture; toss gently to coat. Add greens; toss gently to combine. Spoon tuna salad into pita halves. Makes 4 servings.

Dijon Vinaigrette: In a screw-top jar, combine 2 tablespoons olive oil, 2 tablespoons lime juice, 1 tablespoon Dijon-style mustard, and 1 tablespoon champagne vinegar. Cover; shake well to mix.

Salad Niçoise on Flatbread

With this sophisticated sandwich, you can enjoy all the wonderful flavors of the classic salad in a neat little package.

PER SERVING: 210 cal., 5 g total fat (1 g sat. fat), 24 mg chol., 527 mg sodium, 23 g carb., 3 g fiber, 17 g pro. Exchanges: 1.5 starch, 2.5 very lean meat, 1 fat. Carb choices: 1.5.

- **4 ounces fresh green beans, trimmed (if desired) and cut into 1-inch pieces (about 1 cup)**
- **1 12-ounce can chunk white or light tuna (water-pack), drained and flaked**
- **1 cup halved cherry tomatoes**
- **⅓ cup chopped pitted niçoise or kalamata olives**
- **¼ cup finely chopped sweet onion (such as Vidalia, Walla Walla, or Maui)**
- **2 tablespoons chopped fresh mint**
- **1 tablespoon lemon juice**
- **2 teaspoons olive oil**
- **⅛ teaspoon ground black pepper**
- **3 cups packaged mesclun (mixed salad greens)**
- **3 Greek pita flatbreads**
- **6 short wooden skewers**
- **Cherry tomatoes, pitted niçoise or kalamata olives, and fresh mint leaves**

1. In a covered medium saucepan, cook green beans in boiling water about 4 minutes or until crisp-tender. Drain. Rinse under cold water; drain again.

2. Place green beans in a large bowl. Stir in tuna, the 1 cup cherry tomatoes, the ⅓ cup olives, the onion, and the 2 tablespoons mint. Add lemon juice, oil, and pepper; toss to combine. Stir in mesclun.

3. To serve, cut pita flatbreads in half crosswise. Cut each pita half in half horizontally. Fill each pita half with about ½ cup of the tuna mixture. On each of the wooden skewers, thread a whole cherry tomato, a whole olive, and a mint leaf. Spear each serving with a skewer. Makes 6 servings.

Open-Face Ratatouille Sandwiches

Open-Face Ratatouille Sandwiches

You can save a bundle of carbs by going topless—with your sandwich, that is. A knife and fork will help in eating these sumptuous veggie-packed stacks.

PER SERVING: 251 cal., 7 g total fat (1 g sat. fat), 0 mg chol., 329 mg sodium, 43 g carb., 8 g fiber, 7 g pro. Exchanges: 2 vegetable, 2 starch, 1 fat. Carb choices: 3.

Nonstick cooking spray
- **1 small eggplant, cut into 1-inch pieces**
- **1 small zucchini or yellow summer squash, cut into ¾-inch slices**
- **1 medium red sweet pepper, cut into strips**
- **½ of a small red onion, cut into ½-inch wedges**
- **1 tablespoon olive oil**
- **½ teaspoon herbes de Provence or dried thyme, crushed**
- **¼ teaspoon kosher salt**
- **⅛ teaspoon ground black pepper**
- **2 medium roma tomatoes, each cut lengthwise into 6 wedges**
- **8 small or 4 large ½-inch slices whole wheat or white French bread, toasted**
- **1 clove garlic, halved**
- **2 tablespoons balsamic vinegar**

Fresh thyme sprigs (optional)

1. Preheat oven to 400°F. Coat a large shallow roasting pan with cooking spray. Add eggplant, zucchini, sweet pepper, and red onion to prepared pan. Drizzle with olive oil; sprinkle with herbes de Provence, salt, and black pepper. Toss to coat. Roast vegetables for 30 minutes, tossing once. Add plum tomatoes to roasting pan. Roast for 15 to 20 minutes more or until vegetables are tender and light brown in spots.

2. Meanwhile, rub toasted bread with the cut sides of the garlic clove. Place two small slices or one large slice of the bread on each of four serving plates. Sprinkle balsamic vinegar over vegetables; toss gently to coat. Spoon warm vegetables on top of bread. If desired, garnish with fresh thyme sprigs. Makes 4 servings.

(wrap wonders)

We've all done it. We're in a hurry, so we stop by the fast-food takeout window for a burger and fries. Do you know that it would take less time to make a good-for-you sandwich at home? Keep a few healthful foods on hand just for those busy days. Whole wheat tortillas make a wonderful alternative to bread. Fat-free cream cheese is a flavorful spread that pinch-hits for mainstay mayonnaise. Keep a few veggies on hand, too, such as red sweet peppers and leftover steamed asparagus. Tuna or salmon in a pouch both are a great choices instead of sliced meat.

Salmon and Asparagus Wraps

Start with hot smoked salmon (not lox-style) and coarsely flake it.

PER WRAP: 160 cal., 3 g total fat (1 g sat. fat), 12 mg chol., 555 mg sodium, 20 g carb., 3 g fiber, 13 g pro. Exchanges: 0.5 vegetable, 1 starch, 1.5 very lean meat, 0.5 fat. Carb choices: 1.

- **12 thin fresh asparagus spears**
- **½ of an 8-ounce tub fat-free cream cheese**
- **2 teaspoons finely shredded lemon peel**
- **2 tablespoons lemon juice**
- **⅛ teaspoon cayenne pepper**
- **6 ounces smoked salmon, coarsely flaked and skin and bones removed**
- **¼ cup snipped fresh basil or 2 teaspoons dried basil, crushed**
- **4 6- to 7-inch whole wheat flour tortillas**
- **½ of a red sweet pepper, cut into thin bite-size strips**

1. Snap off and discard woody bases from asparagus. In a covered large saucepan, cook asparagus in a small amount of boiling lightly salted water for 3 to 5 minutes or until crisp-tender. Drain. Plunge into ice water to cool quickly. Drain again; pat dry with paper towels.

2. In a bowl, stir together cream cheese, lemon peel, lemon juice, and cayenne pepper. Fold in smoked salmon and basil.

3. Spread salmon mixture onto tortillas. For each wrap, arrange 3 of the asparagus spears and half of the sweet pepper strips on salmon mixture. Roll up tortillas. If necessary, secure with toothpicks. Makes 4 wraps.

To Make Ahead: Wrap sandwiches in plastic wrap. Chill overnight or until ready to serve.

Salmon and Asparagus Wraps

Smoked Salmon Club Sandwich

Smoked Salmon Club Sandwich

This version reduces the fat, but it definitely does not reduce flavor—chives and red pepper give it plenty.

PER SERVING: 181 cal., 6 g total fat (3 g sat. fat), 17 mg chol., 501 mg sodium, 23 g carb., 2 g fiber, 10 g pro. Exchanges: 0.5 vegetable, 1.5 starch, 0.5 lean meat, 5 fat. Carb choices: 1.5.

- **½ of an 8-ounce package reduced-fat cream cheese (Neufchâtel)**
- **1 small carrot, very finely chopped**
- **1 small zucchini, seeded and very finely chopped**
- **1 small red or yellow sweet pepper, seeded and very finely chopped**
- **2 tablespoons snipped fresh chives**
- **Salt**
- **Ground cayenne pepper**
- **12 slices sesame sourdough bread**
- **2 tablespoons light dairy sour cream**
- **6 ounces thinly sliced smoked salmon**
- **1½ cups baby spinach leaves**
- **1 large cucumber, thinly bias-sliced**

1. For vegetable spread, in a medium bowl, stir together cream cheese, carrot, zucchini, sweet pepper, and chives. Add salt and ground cayenne pepper to taste. If desired, cover and chill for 1 to 24 hours.

2. Spread 4 slices of the bread with dairy sour cream. Arrange salmon on top of sour cream. Add spinach leaves. Spread 4 more slices of the bread with vegetable spread; place on top of sandwich bases, spread sides up. Arrange cucumber slices on spread. Top each sandwich with another slice of bread. Cut sandwiches into quarters. Makes 8 (2-quarter) servings.

Po' Boys

Low-fat coleslaw and baked cornmeal-coated fish give the classic Po' Boy sandwich a delicious, healthful spin.

PER SANDWICH: 345 cal., 13 g total fat (2 g sat. fat), 112 mg chol., 610 mg sodium, 32 g carb., 4 g fiber, 25 g pro. Exchanges: 1 vegetable, 2 starch, 2.5 very lean meat, 1.5 fat. Carb choices: 2.

- **4 4-ounce fresh or frozen gray sole, flounder, or other thin fish fillets**
- **⅓ cup light mayonnaise or salad dressing**
- **1 tablespoon vinegar**
- **1 tablespoon prepared horseradish**
- **1 teaspoon sugar**
- **3 cups packaged shredded cabbage with carrot (coleslaw mix)**
- **1 stalk celery, finely chopped**
- **3 tablespoons chopped fresh parsley**
- **Nonstick cooking spray**
- **1 egg, beaten**
- **1 tablespoon fat-free milk**
- **¼ cup yellow cornmeal**
- **¼ cup fine dry bread crumbs**
- **¼ teaspoon salt**
- **¼ teaspoon ground black pepper**
- **2 teaspoons olive oil**
- **4 whole grain rolls**

1. Preheat oven to 400°F. Thaw fish, if frozen. In a medium bowl, whisk together mayonnaise, vinegar, horseradish, and sugar. Set aside 2 tablespoons of the mixture. Add coleslaw mix, celery, and parsley to the remaining mayonnaise mixture; stir to coat.

2. Rinse fish; pat dry with paper towels. Measure the thickness of fish fillets. Lightly coat a foil-lined shallow baking pan with cooking spray. In a shallow dish, combine egg and milk. In another shallow dish, combine cornmeal, bread crumbs, salt, and pepper; stir in olive oil until well-mixed. Dip fish into egg mixture, then into cornmeal mixture, turning to coat both sides of fish.

3. Place fish in prepared baking pan. Bake for 4 to 6 minutes per ½-inch thickness of fish or until fish flakes easily when tested with a fork.

4. To assemble sandwiches, cut rolls in half and hollow out some of the insides of the top halves; discard crumbs. Spread the reserved 2 tablespoons mayonnaise mixture on the bottom halves of the rolls. Place fish on top. Cover with coleslaw mixture and the top halves of rolls. Makes 4 sandwiches.

Po' Boys

Greek Burgers with Herbed Feta Spread

Oats replace some of the meat in these flavorful burgers, so they're higher in fiber and lower in fat.

PER BURGER: 348 cal., 13 g total fat (5 g sat. fat), 64 mg chol., 585 mg sodium, 31 g carb., 4 g fiber, 27 g pro. Exchanges: 1 vegetable, 1.5 starch, 3 lean meat, 1 fat. Carb choices: 2.

- **12 ounces 90 percent or higher lean ground beef**
- **½ cup quick-cooking rolled oats**
- **⅓ cup finely chopped red onion**
- **1 egg white**
- **3 tablespoons snipped fresh mint or basil**
- **½ teaspoon garlic salt**
- **1 small red sweet pepper, quartered**
- **1 6-ounce carton plain low-fat or fat-free yogurt**
- **⅓ cup crumbled feta cheese with garlic and herb**
- **2 large whole wheat pita bread rounds, halved**
- **1 cup fresh baby spinach leaves**

1. In a medium bowl, combine beef, oats, onion, egg white, 2 tablespoons of the mint, and garlic salt; mix well. Form into four ¾-inch-thick patties.

2. Place patties on the rack of an uncovered grill directly over medium coals. Grill for 12 to 14 minutes or until done (160°F),* turning once. Add pepper quarters to the grill for the last 8 to 10 minutes of grilling or until skins are charred and pepper quarters are tender, turning once.

3. Meanwhile, in a bowl, stir together yogurt and feta cheese. Set aside.

4. If desired, cut grilled pepper quarters into strips, peeling off any loose skin. Serve burgers with pita halves, peppers, feta mixture, and spinach. Top with remaining 1 tablespoon mint. Makes 4 burgers.

***Test Kitchen Tip:** The internal color of a burger is not a reliable doneness indicator. A beef patty cooked to 160°F is safe, regardless of color. To measure the doneness of a patty, insert an instant-read thermometer through the side of the patty to a depth of 2 to 3 inches.

Beef and Black Bean Wraps

Whole wheat tortillas and black beans make this sandwich a filling, high-fiber meal with a spicy flavor.

PER WRAP: 267 cal., 10 g total fat (5 g sat. fat), 44 mg chol., 593 mg sodium, 27 g carb., 14 g fiber, 19 g pro. Exchanges: 1.5 starch, 2 medium-fat meat. Carb choices: 2.

- **8 ounces lean ground beef**
- **1 cup chopped onion**
- **2 cloves garlic, minced**
- **1½ teaspoons ground cumin**
- **1 teaspoon chili powder**
- **½ teaspoon ground coriander**
- **1 15-ounce can black beans, rinsed and drained**
- **1 large tomato, chopped**
- **¼ teaspoon salt**
- **¼ teaspoon ground black pepper**
- **6 8-inch whole wheat flour tortillas**
- **1½ cups shredded lettuce**
- **1 to 1½ cups shredded cheddar or Monterey Jack cheese (4 to 6 ounces)**
- **Purchased salsa (optional)**

1. In a large skillet, cook ground beef, onion, and garlic about 5 minutes or until meat is brown. Drain off fat.

2. Stir cumin, chili powder, and coriander into meat mixture in skillet. Cook and stir for 1 minute. Stir in beans, tomato, salt, and pepper. Cover; cook for 5 minutes more, stirring occasionally.

3. To serve, spoon some of the beef mixture down the center of each tortilla. Sprinkle with lettuce and cheese. Roll up. If desired, serve with salsa. Makes 6 wraps.

Greek Burgers with Herbed Feta Spread

Pork Primavera Sandwiches

This slow-cooker recipe can be put on to cook (on low) at lunchtime and will be ready when you get home from work.

PER SANDWICH: 258 cal., 5 g total fat (1 g sat. fat), 57 mg chol., 418 mg sodium, 28 g carb., 3 g fiber, 24 g pro. Exchanges: 2 starch, 2.5 medium-fat meat. Carb choices: 2.

- **2 medium carrots, shredded (about 1 cup)**
- **1 large red sweet pepper, seeded and coarsely chopped**
- **1 medium onion, cut into thin wedges**
- **2 tablespoons quick-cooking tapioca, crushed**
- **2 to 2½ pounds boneless pork sirloin roast or boneless pork loin roast, trimmed of fat**
- **¾ cup bottled reduced-sodium, fat-free barbecue sauce**
- **10 whole wheat hamburger buns, split and toasted**

1. In a 3½- or 4-quart slow cooker, combine carrots, sweet pepper, and onion. Sprinkle with tapioca. Place pork roast on top of vegetables. Pour barbecue sauce over meat. Cover and cook on low-heat setting for 6 to 7 hours or on high-heat setting for 3 to 3½ hours.

2. Remove meat from slow cooker, reserving juices. Thinly slice meat. Return sliced meat to slow cooker; stir to coat with sauce. Serve meat on hamburger buns. Makes 10 sandwiches.

Beef and Sweet Pepper Tortilla Wraps

If you have more wraps than you need, cut an extra one into small pieces for a midafternoon snack.

PER WRAP: 135 cal., 6 g total fat (3 g sat. fat), 24 mg chol., 186 mg sodium, 10 g carb., 1 g fiber, 8 g pro. Exchanges: 0.5 starch, 1 lean meat, 0.5 fat. Carb choices: 0.5.

- **3 7- or 8-inch flour tortillas**
- **½ of an 8-ounce tub light cream cheese with chive and onion or roasted garlic**
- **18 to 24 fresh basil leaves**
- **½ of a 7-ounce jar roasted red sweet peppers, well-drained and cut into ¼-inch strips**
- **4 ounces thinly sliced cooked beef, ham, and/or turkey**
- **1 tablespoon low-fat or light mayonnaise or salad dressing**

1. Spread each tortilla with one-third of the cream cheese. Cover each with basil leaves, leaving a 1-inch border. Arrange pepper strips on basil leaves. Top with sliced meat. Spread mayonnaise onto meat.

2. Tightly roll up each tortilla into a spiral; cut each wrap in half crosswise. Makes 6 wraps.

Make-Ahead Directions: Wrap each spiral in plastic wrap. Chill for up to 4 hours.

Bacon, Lettuce, and Tomato Salsa Wraps

Bacon, Lettuce, and Tomato Salsa Wraps

Homemade fresh tomato salsa makes this healthful version of the BLT a cut above the rest.

PER SERVING: 227 cal., 9 g total fat (3 g sat. fat), 30 mg chol., 625 mg sodium, 27 g carb., 2 g fiber, 8 g pro. Exchanges: 1 vegetable, 1.5 starch, 0.5 medium-fat meat, 1.5 fat. Carb choices: 2.

2 large ripe tomatoes, seeded and coarsely chopped
¼ cup finely chopped red onion
¼ cup chopped fresh cilantro
1 tablespoon finely chopped fresh jalapeño chile pepper*
1 tablespoon lime juice
⅛ teaspoon kosher salt
8 slices turkey bacon or reduced-sodium turkey bacon
¼ cup light mayonnaise or salad dressing
4 10-inch vegetable-flavor flour tortillas or flour tortillas
2 cups fresh baby spinach

1. For salsa, in a medium bowl, combine tomatoes, red onion, cilantro, and chile pepper. Stir in lime juice and salt. Set aside.

2. Cook bacon according to package directions. Drain well on paper towels; cut bacon into large pieces.

3. To assemble wraps, spread mayonnaise over tortillas; top with spinach. Using a slotted spoon, spoon salsa over spinach. Top with bacon. Roll up tortillas. Cut each tortilla in half. Makes 4 (2-wrap-half) servings.

***Test Kitchen Tip:** Because chile peppers contain volatile oils that can burn your skin and eyes, avoid direct contact with them as much as possible. When working with chile peppers, wear plastic or rubber gloves. If your bare hands do touch the peppers, wash your hands and nails well with soap and warm water.

Fast Fajita Roll-Ups

Plan this meal-in-a-bundle for those busy nights when you have little time to cook. It takes just 20 minutes.

PER ROLL-UP: 280 cal., 11 g total fat (5 g sat. fat), 42 mg chol., 425 mg sodium, 19 g carb., 1 g fiber, 25 g pro. Exchanges: 1 starch, 3 lean meat, 0.5 fat. Carb choices: 1.

12 ounces beef flank steak or sirloin steak or skinless, boneless chicken breast halves
4 8-inch whole wheat, spinach, or flour tortillas
Nonstick cooking spray
⅓ cup finely chopped onion
⅓ cup finely chopped green sweet pepper
½ cup chopped tomato
2 tablespoons bottled fat-free Italian salad dressing
½ cup shredded reduced-fat cheddar cheese (2 ounces)
¼ cup purchased salsa or bottled taco sauce
¼ cup light dairy sour cream (optional)

1. If desired, partially freeze beef for easier slicing. If using beef, trim fat from meat. Cut beef or chicken into bite-size strips.

2. Preheat oven to 350°F. Wrap tortillas tightly in foil. Heat in oven about 10 minutes or until tortillas are heated through.

3. Meanwhile, coat an unheated 12-inch nonstick skillet with cooking spray. Preheat over medium-high heat. Add meat, onion, and sweet pepper to hot skillet. Cook and stir for 2 to 3 minutes or until desired doneness for beef or until chicken is no longer pink. Remove from heat; drain well. Stir in tomato and salad dressing.

4. To serve, fill warm tortillas with meat mixture. Roll up tortillas. Serve with cheese, salsa, and, if desired, sour cream. Makes 4 roll-ups.

Roast Beef and Red Pepper Sandwiches

A combination of Dijon-style mustard, horseradish, and mayonnaise adds a flavor punch to this not-so-ordinary roast beef sandwich.

PER SANDWICH: 210 cal., 8 g total fat (3 g sat. fat), 38 mg chol., 312 mg sodium, 14 g carb., 1 g fiber, 20 g pro. Exchanges: 1 starch, 2.5 lean meat, 1 fat. Carb choices: 1.

- **1 4-ounce package 8-inch Italian bread shells (2 shells) (such as Boboli brand)**
- **1½ teaspoons light mayonnaise or salad dressing**
- **1½ teaspoons Dijon-style mustard**
- **½ to 1 teaspoon prepared horseradish**
- **6 ounces thinly sliced cooked roast beef**
- **¼ cup bottled roasted red sweet peppers, cut into ¼-inch strips**
- **2 ounces thinly sliced Monterey Jack cheese**
- **2 cups watercress, tough stems removed**

1. Preheat oven to 350°F. Wrap bread shells tightly in foil. Bake for 10 minutes or until warmed through.

2. In a small bowl, combine mayonnaise, mustard, and horseradish. Spread one side of each bread shell with mayonnaise mixture. Top each with roast beef, sweet pepper strips, cheese, and watercress. Fold bread in half over filling or roll wrap-style. Slice each in half crosswise to serve. Makes 4 sandwiches.

Make-Ahead Directions: Wrap sandwiches tightly in plastic wrap and refrigerate for up to 24 hours.

Curried Chicken Salad Wraps

Tex-Mex Sloppy Joes

Sloppy joes or other types of loose-meat sandwiches are standard fare in many cafes. This recipe gives the popular meal-in-a-bun a twist by using ground chicken or turkey breast instead of ground beef.

PER SANDWICH: 280 cal., 6 g total fat (1 g sat. fat), 44 mg chol., 644 mg sodium, 35 g carb., 4 g fiber, 23 g pro. Exchanges: 1 vegetable, 2 starch, 2 very lean meat, ½ fat. Carb choices: 2.

2 teaspoons cooking oil
2 medium onions, chopped
1 medium green sweet pepper, chopped
½ cup fresh or frozen whole kernel corn
2 large cloves garlic, minced
1 fresh jalapeño chile pepper, seeded (if desired) and finely chopped*
1 pound uncooked ground chicken breast or turkey breast
1 teaspoon chili powder
1 teaspoon ground cumin
1 teaspoon dried oregano, crushed
¾ cup ketchup
4 teaspoons Worcestershire sauce
6 whole grain sandwich-style rolls
Dill pickle slices (optional)

1. In a very large nonstick skillet, heat oil over medium-high heat. Add onions, sweet pepper, corn, garlic, and chile pepper. Cook for 4 to 5 minutes or until onions are tender, stirring occasionally. Stir in chicken or turkey, chili powder, cumin, and oregano. Cook for 5 to 6 minutes more or until chicken or turkey is no longer pink. Stir in ketchup and Worcestershire sauce; heat through.

2. Divide mixture among rolls. If desired, top with pickle slices. Makes 6 sandwiches.

***Test Kitchen Tip:** Because chile peppers contain volatile oils that can burn your skin and eyes, avoid direct contact with them as much as possible. When working with chile peppers, wear plastic or rubber gloves. If your bare hands do touch the peppers, wash your hands and nails well with soap and warm water.

Curried Chicken Salad Wraps

You can serve the chicken filling stuffed in tomatoes instead of rolled in tortillas, if you like.

PER WRAP: 246 cal., 5 g total fat (1 g sat. fat), 60 mg chol., 537 mg sodium, 18 g carb., 9 g fiber, 28 g pro. Exchanges: 1 vegetable, 1 starch, 3 very lean meat, 0.5 fat. Carb choices: 1.

½ cup fat-free or low-fat mayonnaise or salad dressing
½ teaspoon curry powder
⅛ teaspoon ground black pepper
2 cups chopped cooked chicken breast (about 10 ounces)
¼ cup sliced green onions
4 7-inch whole wheat flour tortillas
4 romaine leaves or 8 fresh spinach leaves
1 medium tomato, chopped

1. In a medium bowl, combine mayonnaise, curry powder, and pepper. Stir in chicken and green onions. If desired, cover and chill for 2 to 24 hours.

2. Top tortillas with leaves, chicken mixture, and tomato. Roll up. Makes 4 wraps.

Grilled Chicken Sandwiches

A little lime punches up the flavor in the fat-free dressing.

PER SANDWICH: 259 cal., 2 g total fat (0 g sat. fat), 66 mg chol., 488 mg sodium, 27 g carb., 3 g fiber, 31 g pro. Exchanges: 0.5 vegetable, 1.5 starch, 4 very lean meat. Carb choices: 2.

- **¼ cup fat-free mayonnaise or salad dressing**
- **½ teaspoon finely shredded lime peel or lemon peel**
- **1 medium zucchini or yellow summer squash, cut lengthwise into ¼-inch slices**
- **3 tablespoons Worcestershire sauce**
- **4 skinless, boneless chicken breast halves (1 to 1¼ pounds total)**
- **4 whole wheat hamburger buns, split and toasted**

1. In a small bowl, combine mayonnaise and lime peel. Cover and chill until serving time.

2. Brush zucchini slices with 1 tablespoon of the Worcestershire sauce; set aside. Brush chicken with remaining 2 tablespoons Worcestershire sauce.

3. Place chicken on the rack of an uncovered grill directly over medium coals. Grill chicken for 12 to 15 minutes, adding zucchini the last 6 minutes. Grill until chicken is no longer pink (170°F) and zucchini is tender, turning once.

4. To serve, spread lime dressing onto cut sides of toasted buns. If desired, cut zucchini slices in half crosswise. Place chicken and zucchini slices on bun bottoms; add bun tops. Makes 4 sandwiches.

Grilled Chicken Sandwiches

Sesame-Ginger Turkey Wraps

A fruit salad to accompany these irresistible Asian-inspired slow-cooker wraps would make a delectable dinner.

PER WRAP: 207 cal., 5 g total fat (1 g sat. fat), 67 mg chol., 422 mg sodium, 20 g carb., 2 g fiber, 20 g pro. Exchanges: 1 vegetable, 1 starch, 2 lean meat. Carb choices: 1.5.

- **Nonstick cooking spray**
- **3 turkey thighs, skinned (3½ to 4 pounds total)**
- **1 cup bottled sesame-ginger stir-fry sauce**
- **¼ cup water**
- **1 16-ounce package shredded broccoli (broccoli slaw mix)**
- **12 8-inch flour tortillas, warmed***
- **¾ cup sliced green onions**

1. Lightly coat a 3½- or 4-quart slow cooker with cooking spray. Place turkey thighs in slow cooker. In a small bowl, stir together stir-fry sauce and the water. Pour over turkey.

2. Cover and cook on low-heat setting for 6 to 7 hours or on high-heat setting for 3 to 3½ hours.

3. Remove turkey from slow cooker; cool slightly. Remove turkey from bones; discard bones. Using two forks, pull turkey apart into shreds.

4. Meanwhile, place broccoli in the sauce mixture in the slow cooker; stir to coat. Cover and let stand for 5 minutes. Using a slotted spoon, remove broccoli from slow cooker.

5. To assemble, place some of the turkey on each tortilla. Top with broccoli mixture and green onions. Spoon sauce from slow cooker on top of green onions. Roll up. Serve immediately. Makes 12 wraps.

***Test Kitchen Tip:** To warm tortillas, wrap them in white microwave-safe paper towels; microwave on 100 percent power (high) for 15 to 30 seconds or until tortillas are softened. (Or preheat oven to 350°F. Wrap tortillas in foil. Heat for 10 to 15 minutes or until warmed.)

Grilled Turkey Burgers with Curry Mustard

Surprise your palate with the flavor of curry and mustard in every bite of these burgers.

PER BURGER: 265 cal., 8 g total fat (2 g sat. fat), 68 mg chol., 428 mg sodium, 26 g carb., 3 g fiber, 20 g pro. Exchanges: 2 starch, 2 lean meat. Carb choices: 2.

½ cup finely shredded carrot
¼ cup thinly sliced green onions
¼ cup soft whole wheat bread crumbs
2 tablespoons milk
¼ teaspoon dried Italian seasoning, crushed
¼ teaspoon garlic salt
Dash ground black pepper
¾ pound uncooked ground turkey or chicken
4 whole wheat hamburger buns, split and toasted
Shredded zucchini (optional)
Sliced tomato (optional)
1 recipe Curry Mustard (see recipe, below) (optional)

1. In a medium bowl, stir together carrot, green onions, bread crumbs, milk, Italian seasoning, garlic salt, and pepper. Add ground turkey or chicken; mix well. Shape meat mixture into four ½-inch-thick patties.

2. Grill burgers on the rack of an uncovered grill directly over medium coals for 14 to 18 minutes or until an instant-read thermometer inserted into the center of burgers registers 160°F,* turning once halfway through grilling. (Or place burgers on unheated rack of a broiler pan. Broil 3 to 4 inches from heat for 12 to 14 minutes or until done, turning once.)

3. To serve, place burgers on buns. If desired, serve burgers with zucchini, tomato, and Curry Mustard. Makes 4 burgers.

Curry Mustard: In a small bowl, stir together ¼ cup Dijon-style mustard and ½ teaspoon curry powder. Makes ¼ cup.

***Test Kitchen Tip:** The internal color of a burger is not a reliable indication of doneness. A turkey patty cooked to 165°F is safe, regardless of color. To check, insert an instant-read thermometer into side to a depth of 2 to 3 inches.

Thai Turkey Burgers

Thai Turkey Burgers

Subbing small buns for big ones and mango slices for cheese lets burgers stay on your A-OK list.

PER BURGER: 213 cal., 4 g total fat (1 g sat. fat), 30 mg chol., 438 mg sodium, 23 g carb., 2 g fiber, 22 g pro. Exchanges: 1 starch, 0.5 fruit, 3 very lean meat. Carb choices: 1.5.

¼ cup refrigerated or frozen egg product, thawed, or 1 egg, beaten
¼ cup fine dry bread crumbs
1 teaspoon Thai seasoning or curry powder
1 pound uncooked ground turkey breast
6 small whole grain buns, split and toasted
¾ cup fresh basil
2 tablespoons bottled peanut sauce
1 medium mango, pitted, peeled, and sliced

1. In a medium bowl, combine egg, bread crumbs, and Thai seasoning. Add turkey; mix well. Shape into six ¾-inch-thick patties.

2. Grill patties on greased rack of an uncovered grill directly over medium heat for 14 to 18 minutes or until done (165°F),* turning once.

3. Top each bun bottom with basil, patty, peanut sauce, mango, and bun top. Makes 6 burgers.

***Test Kitchen Tip:** The internal color of a burger is not a reliable indication of doneness. A turkey patty cooked to 165°F is safe, regardless of color. To check, insert an instant-read thermometer into side to a depth of 2 to 3 inches.

Cheese and Tomato Stack

Fresh summer basil and tomatoes take a cheese sandwich from ordinary to fantastic.

PER SANDWICH: 203 cal., 12 g total fat (4 g sat. fat), 22 mg chol., 531 mg sodium, 16 g carb., 3 g fiber, 10 g pro. Exchanges: 1 starch, 1 medium-fat meat, 0.5 vegetable, 1 fat. Carb choices: 1.

- **2 whole wheat English muffin, toasted**
- **8 thin red and/or yellow tomato slices**
- **4 ounces fresh mozzarella, cut into 4 slices**
- **4 teaspoons snipped fresh basil**
- **4 teaspoons olive oil**
- **¼ teaspoon salt**
- **¼ teaspoon cracked black pepper**
- **4 grape tomatoes or cherry tomatoes, halved (optional)**

1. For each serving, on one English muffin half, layer a tomato slice, a mozzarella slice, and ½ teaspoon of the basil. Repeat layers. In a small bowl, combine olive oil, salt, and pepper. Drizzle over top. If desired, top with grape tomato halves. Makes 4 open-face sandwiches.

simple sides and salads

Creamy Potato Salad

Often what makes the meal is not the food at the center of the plate but the array of sides. The trick is serving dishes that keep carbs and fat in check. Here, you'll find healthful ideas to round out the meal: whole grain pilaf, veggie and fruit salads, grilled vegetables, and more.

Creamy Potato Salad

This flavorful potato salad will make you feel like you're not missing out on a summer favorite.

PER SERVING: 153 cal., 7 g total fat (2 g sat. fat), 52 mg chol., 261 mg sodium, 18 g carb., 2 g fiber, 6 g pro. Exchanges: 1 starch, 0.5 lean meat, 1 fat. Carb choices: 1.

2½ pounds round white and/or red potatoes
1 cup low-fat or light mayonnaise dressing or salad dressing
1 8-ounce carton light dairy sour cream
2 tablespoons fat-free milk
1 teaspoon seasoned pepper
¼ teaspoon salt
3 hard-cooked eggs, peeled and cut up
¾ cup sliced green onions
½ cup cubed reduced-fat cheddar cheese (2 ounces)
4 slices bacon or turkey bacon, crisp-cooked and crumbled
1 medium avocado

1. In a covered large saucepan, cook potatoes in a large amount of boiling water for 20 to 25 minutes or just until tender. Drain and cool. Cut into bite-size cubes.
2. In a very large storage container or serving bowl, stir together mayonnaise, sour cream, milk, seasoned pepper, and salt. Gently stir in cubed potatoes, hard-cooked eggs, green onions, and cheese. Cover potato mixture and chill for 2 to 24 hours. Cover and chill bacon separately.
3. Before serving, if salad seems dry, stir in 1 to 2 tablespoons additional milk.
4. To serve, seed, peel, and chop avocado; stir into salad. Sprinkle salad with crumbled bacon. Makes 16 servings.

Quick Tip:

When you have a side dish—like Blue Cheese-Stuffed Summer Squash—that will wow your dinner companions, a simple meat entrée will suffice. Grill a pork chop, broil a tenderloin steak, or caramelize a piece of fresh salmon in a skillet for a very satisfying meal.

Blue Cheese-Stuffed Summer Squash

Basil and Tomato Pasta Salad

Blue Cheese-Stuffed Summer Squash

Piquant blue cheese does contain fat, but it has such big flavor, you only need a little bit.

PER SERVING: 107 cal., 6 g total fat (3 g sat. fat), 15 mg chol., 178 mg sodium, 8 g carb., 1 g fiber, 5 g pro. Exchanges: 0.5 high-fat meat, 1 vegetable, 0.5 fat. Carb choices: 0.5.

Nonstick cooking spray
4 medium yellow summer squash and/or zucchini
½ of an 8-ounce package reduced-fat cream cheese (Neufchâtel), softened
½ cup shredded carrot
⅓ cup crumbled blue cheese
⅓ cup thinly sliced green onions
⅓ cup fine dry bread crumbs
¼ cup fat-free or light dairy sour cream
⅛ teaspoon ground black pepper
2 tablespoons chopped walnuts

1. Preheat oven to 400°F. Coat a 3-quart rectangular baking dish with cooking spray; set aside.

2. Halve the squash lengthwise. Remove seeds with a spoon, leaving a shell about ¼ inch thick. Place squash halves, cut sides down, in prepared baking dish. Bake, uncovered, for 10 minutes. Turn squash halves cut sides up.

3. Meanwhile, for filling, in a medium bowl, stir together cream cheese, carrot, blue cheese, green onions, ¼ cup of the bread crumbs, sour cream, and pepper (the mixture will be stiff).

4. Spoon filling evenly into squash halves. Top with walnuts and remaining bread crumbs. Bake, uncovered, about 10 minutes or until squash is tender and filling is heated through. Makes 8 servings.

Make-Ahead Directions: Prepare as directed through Step 3. Cover and chill for up to 24 hours. Bake as directed in Step 4, except bake about 15 minutes.

Basil and Tomato Pasta Salad

If you use dried herbs, chill the salad at least two hours so they rehydrate.

PER SERVING: 152 cal., 4 g total fat (1 g sat. fat), 4 mg chol., 161 mg sodium, 23 g carb., 1 g fiber, 6 g pro. Exchanges: 1.5 starch, 0.5 fat. Carb choices: 1.5.

1 pound dried gemelli pasta
1 pound red and/or yellow tomatoes, chopped
1 cup shredded reduced-fat mozzarella cheese (4 ounces)
½ cup thinly sliced red onion
½ cup quartered pitted kalamata or ripe olives
¼ cup thinly sliced fresh basil or 4 teaspoons dried basil, crushed
2 tablespoons snipped fresh oregano or 2 teaspoons dried oregano, crushed
2 tablespoons capers, rinsed and drained
2 cloves garlic, minced
2 tablespoons olive oil

1. Cook pasta according to package directions. Drain; rinse under cold water. Drain again.

2. In a large bowl, combine pasta, tomatoes, cheese, onion, olives, basil, oregano, capers, garlic, ¼ teaspoon *salt,* and ⅛ teaspoon ground black *pepper.* Add oil; toss gently to mix. Cover and chill for 2 to 4 hours. Makes 16 (¾-cup) servings.

Tomatoes with Crispy Bread Topping

Thyme supplies a strong, somewhat minty flavor to these roasted tomatoes.

PER SERVING: 75 cal., 4 g total fat (1 g sat. fat), 0 mg chol., 152 mg sodium, 9 g carb., 3 g fiber, 2 g pro. Exchanges: 1.5 vegetable, 1 fat. Carb choices: 0.5.

- **8 roma tomatoes, cored and cut in half lengthwise**
- **Kosher salt**
- **Freshly ground black pepper**
- **½ cup soft whole wheat bread crumbs**
- **¼ cup thinly sliced green onions**
- **2 tablespoons chopped fresh thyme**
- **1 tablespoon chopped fresh flat-leaf parsley**
- **1 tablespoon chopped fresh tarragon**
- **1 tablespoon extra virgin olive oil**
- **2 cloves garlic, minced**

1. Preheat oven to 400°F. Sprinkle the cut sides of the tomatoes with kosher salt and pepper. Arrange tomatoes, cut sides up, in a shallow baking pan. Set aside.

2. In a small bowl, combine bread crumbs, green onions, thyme, parsley, tarragon, olive oil, and garlic.* Sprinkle atop tomato halves. Bake, uncovered, for 15 to 20 minutes or until the tomatoes are heated through and the bread crumbs are browned and crisp. Makes 4 (2-half) servings.

***Note:** If desired, add 1 tablespoon grated Parmesan cheese to the bread crumb topping.

Mint-Buttered Soybeans

Fresh or frozen soybeans, sometimes labeled as edamame, in pods or shelled can be found at health food stores or in the health food section of the supermarket.

PER SERVING: 139 cal., 7 g total fat (1 g sat. fat), 4 mg chol., 119 mg sodium, 10 g carb., 4 g fiber, 11 g pro. Exchanges: 0.5 starch, 1.5 very lean meat, 1 fat. Carb choices: 0.5.

- **2 teaspoons butter**
- **3 cups shelled fresh or frozen sweet soybeans (edamame), thawed**
- **3 tablespoons snipped fresh mint**
- **1 tablespoon snipped fresh basil**
- **¼ teaspoon salt**

Tomatoes with Crispy Bread Topping

1. In a medium skillet, melt butter over medium heat. Add soybeans; cook and stir about 5 minutes or until soybeans are tender.

2. Stir mint, snipped basil, and salt into soybeans. Makes 6 (½-cup) servings.

Tex-Mex Black-Eyed Pea Medley

Black-eyed peas are the stars in this spicy combo. Take it to your next potluck or halve the recipe for fewer servings.

PER SERVING: 34 cal., 0 g total fat, 1 mg chol., 223 mg sodium, 6 g carb., 1 g fiber, 2 g pro. Exchanges: 0.5 starch. Carb choices: 0.5.

- **1 cup sliced green onions or finely chopped onion**
- **¾ cup finely chopped red or green sweet pepper**
- **1 4-ounce can diced green chile peppers, drained**
- **½ cup purchased salsa**
- **½ cup bottled reduced-calorie Italian salad dressing**
- **3 cloves garlic, minced**
- **⅛ teaspoon ground black pepper**
- **Few dashes bottled hot pepper sauce**
- **1 15-ounce can black-eyed peas, rinsed and drained***

1. In a large bowl, combine onions, sweet pepper, chile peppers, salsa, salad dressing, garlic, black pepper, and hot pepper sauce. Stir in black-eyed peas. Cover; chill for 3 to 24 hours. Makes 14 (about ¼-cup) servings.

***Note:** If you prefer, you can substitute ½ of a 16-ounce package frozen black-eyed peas (about 1⅔ cups) for the canned peas. Cook the frozen peas according to package directions. Drain, then rinse in a colander.

(choosing sides)

You choose the entrée for your meals with the utmost care. But if you slather your sides with butter and oil or overcook them, the care you've taken with the main dish is for naught! Vegetables are only as nutritious as your preparation techniques. If you cook a vegetable until it is limp, you've stripped it of its vitamins. Steamed or lightly sautéed veggies that are still a bit firm to the bite are not only tastier but retain their vital nutrients as well. So the next time you serve a vegetable along with your main dish, choose your cooking technique wisely.

Mint-Buttered Soybeans

(10 easy sides)

Looking for a great side? Here are 10 to count on.

1. **Roast** a garlic head until soft. Mash the peeled cloves into cooked mashed potatoes.
2. **Prepare** a purchased brown rice pilaf mix; stir in shredded carrot, sliced mushrooms, and snipped fresh basil.
3. **Stir** a small amount of pesto into mashed potatoes or cooked pasta.
4. **Cut** purchased polenta into ½-inch slices and broil until crispy. Serve sprinkled with Parmesan cheese.
5. **Toss** cut-up zucchini, onion, and red sweet pepper with a little olive oil and grill in a grill wok until tender.
6. **Steam** unseasoned mixed vegetables and toss with snipped fresh oregano and a squeeze of fresh lemon.
7. **Toss** cut-up carrots, onion, and parsnips with a little walnut oil and balsamic vinegar; roast until tender.
8. **Cook** baby carrots in a small amount of chicken broth and sprinkle with curry powder.
9. **Steam** broccoli florets. Drizzle with toasted sesame oil and sprinkle with some sesame seeds.
10. **Roast** small new potatoes with a little olive oil, minced garlic, and snipped fresh rosemary. Add halved cherry tomatoes the last 5 minutes of roasting.

Cheesy Squash Bake

Cheesy Squash Bake

A creamy low-fat cheese sauce dresses up this squash side dish for fewer calories than you'd think.

PER SERVING: 72 cal., 3 g total fat (1 g sat. fat), 7 mg chol., 169 mg sodium, 8 g carb., 1 g fiber, 5 g pro. Exchanges: 1 vegetable, 0.5 medium-fat meat. Carb choices: 0.5.

- **1 pound yellow summer squash, sliced**
- **½ cup chopped onion**
- **1 tablespoon reduced-fat margarine**
- **1 tablespoon all-purpose flour**
- **½ cup fat-free milk**
- **½ cup shredded reduced-fat cheddar cheese (2 ounces)**
- **¼ teaspoon ground black pepper**
- **⅛ teaspoon salt**
- **Nonstick cooking spray**
- **½ cup soft whole wheat bread crumbs, toasted**

1. Preheat oven to 350°F. In a large saucepan, cook squash and onion in a small amount of boiling water for 5 to 10 minutes or until tender; drain and set aside.

2. Meanwhile, in a medium saucepan, melt margarine over medium heat. Stir in flour. Add milk all at once; cook and stir until mixture is thickened and bubbly. Remove from heat. Add shredded cheese, pepper, and salt; stir until cheese is melted. Add the drained squash mixture; toss gently to coat the vegetables.

3. Coat a 1- to 1½-quart baking dish, casserole, or soufflé dish with cooking spray. Spoon the squash mixture into the prepared dish. Sprinkle bread crumbs evenly onto vegetables. Bake about 25 minutes or until the top is golden and the mixture is heated through. Makes 6 (½-cup) servings.

Red Lentil, Quinoa, and Flaxseed Pilaf

Red lentils and quinoa boost the fiber in this side or vegetarian main dish. Look for them with the beans and grains at your supermarket.

PER SIDE-DISH SERVING: 152 cal., 5 g total fat (1 g sat. fat), 0 mg chol., 198 mg sodium, 20 g carb., 4 g fiber, 7 g pro. Exchanges: 1.5 starch, 1 fat. Carb choices: 1.

- **⅓ cup dry red lentils**
- **⅓ cup quinoa**
- **1 tablespoon olive oil**
- **⅓ cup finely chopped shallots or onion**
- **2 cloves garlic, minced**

Red Lentil, Quinoa, and Flaxseed Pilaf

- **2 tablespoons flaxseeds**
- **1 14-ounce can reduced-sodium chicken broth**
- **1 large red or green sweet pepper, chopped**
- **1 teaspoon snipped fresh thyme or ¼ teaspoon dried thyme, crushed**
- **Fresh thyme sprigs (optional)**

1. Rinse and drain lentils and quinoa separately. In a medium saucepan, heat olive oil over medium heat. Add shallots and garlic; cook and stir for 3 minutes.

2. Add quinoa and flaxseeds to shallot mixture in pan; cook and stir about 5 minutes or until the quinoa is light brown.

3. Add lentils and chicken broth to quinoa mixture. Bring to boiling; reduce heat. Cover and simmer for 15 minutes.

4. Stir in sweet pepper and snipped or dried thyme. Cover and cook about 5 minutes more or until quinoa and lentils are tender. Let stand, covered, for 5 minutes. If desired, garnish with thyme sprigs. Makes 5 (½-cup) side-dish or 2 (1¼-cup) main-dish servings

Thyme-Roasted Asparagus

Thyme-Roasted Asparagus

Bake tender asparagus spears in a little thyme-laced olive oil.

PER SERVING: 110 cal., 9 g total fat (2 g sat. fat), 5 mg chol., 269 mg sodium, 5 g carb., 2 g fiber, 4 g pro. Exchanges: 1 vegetable, 2 fat. Carb choices: 0.

2 tablespoons olive oil
1 teaspoon snipped fresh thyme or ½ teaspoon dried thyme, crushed
¼ teaspoon salt
¼ teaspoon ground black pepper
1 pound fresh asparagus spears, trimmed
½ cup roasted red pepper strips
¼ cup shaved Parmesan cheese (1 ounce)
2 tablespoons snipped fresh parsley

1. Preheat oven to 400°F. In a small bowl, combine oil, thyme, salt, and black pepper; pour over asparagus. Toss gently to coat.

2. Arrange asparagus spears in a single layer in a 15×10×1-inch baking pan. Bake, uncovered, for 10 to 12 minutes or until tender, turning spears once.

3. Top with pepper strips, Parmesan, and parsley. Makes 4 servings.

Green Bean Salad

Keep some of the homemade vinaigrette in the refrigerator to perk up tossed green salads.

PER SERVING: 53 cal., 2 g total fat (0 g sat. fat), 0 mg chol., 126 mg sodium, 8 g carb., 3 g fiber, 2 g pro. Exchanges: 1.5 vegetable, 0.5 fat. Carb choices: 0.5.

12 ounces fresh green beans, trimmed
8 ounces yellow and/or red cherry tomatoes, halved
½ of a small red onion, thinly sliced
1 recipe Basil-Tomato Vinaigrette (see recipe, below)

1. In a medium saucepan, cook green beans, covered, in a small amount of boiling lightly salted water about 8 minutes or just until crisp-tender. Drain; rinse with cold water and drain again.

2. In a large bowl, combine beans, cherry tomato halves, and red onion slices. Drizzle with Basil-Tomato Vinaigrette; toss gently to coat. Cover and chill before serving. Makes 6 (about ¾-cup) servings.

Basil-Tomato Vinaigrette: In a screw-top jar, combine ⅓ cup snipped fresh basil, 3 tablespoons red wine vinegar, 2 tablespoons snipped dried tomatoes,* 1 tablespoon olive oil, 2 cloves minced garlic, ¼ teaspoon salt, and ¼ teaspoon ground black pepper. Cover; shake to mix. Chill until ready to use. Makes about ⅔ cup.

***Test Kitchen Tip:** To soften dried tomatoes for the vinaigrette, soak them in enough boiling water to cover for 5 minutes; drain well.

Make-Ahead Directions: Prepare Basil-Tomato Vinaigrette as directed. Cover and chill for up to 8 hours. Shake before using.

Quick Tip:

Eating healthful foods doesn't mean forgoing flavor. Herbs pack a lot of concentrated flavor punch into a recipe without adding fat and very few calories. For the best results, toss snipped or minced fresh herbs into the final dish just before serving.

Green Bean Salad

Chipotle Coleslaw

This recipe calls for ground chipotle chile pepper, which gives the coleslaw a spicy kick.

PER SERVING: 55 cal., 1 g total fat (0 g sat. fat), 1 mg chol., 122 mg sodium, 13 g carb., 2 g fiber, 2 g pro. Exchanges: 2 vegetable. Carb choices: 1.

- **⅓ cup fat-free mayonnaise**
- **1 tablespoon lime juice**
- **2 teaspoons honey**
- **¼ teaspoon ground cumin**
- **⅛ to ¼ teaspoon ground chipotle chile pepper**
- **3 cups shredded green cabbage**
- **¾ cup whole kernel corn, thawed if frozen**
- **¾ cup chopped red sweet pepper**
- **⅓ cup thinly sliced red onion**
- **⅓ cup chopped cilantro**

1. In a small bowl, stir together mayonnaise, lime juice, honey, cumin, and chipotle chile pepper.

2. In a large bowl, combine cabbage, corn, sweet pepper, onion, and cilantro. Pour mayonnaise mixture over cabbage mixture. Toss lightly to coat. Serve immediately or cover and chill up to 24 hours. Makes 6 (⅔-cup) servings.

Pepper and Four-Bean Salad

Pepper and Four-Bean Salad

More vinegar than oil in the tarragon marinade lowers the fat—but not the zippy flavor.

PER SERVING: 117 cal., 4 g total fat (0 g sat. fat), 0 mg chol., 146 mg sodium, 17 g carb., 5 g fiber, 5 g pro. Exchanges: 1.5 vegetable, 0.5 starch, 1 fat. Carb choices: 1.

PER SERVING WITH SUBSTITUTE: same as above, except 114 cal., 16 g carb.

- **4 cups trimmed 1½-inch pieces fresh green beans and/or wax beans or one 16-ounce package frozen cut green beans**
- **1 15- to 16-ounce can kidney beans, rinsed and drained**
- **1 15- to 16-ounce can garbanzo beans (chickpeas), rinsed and drained**
- **3 medium green, red, and/or yellow sweet peppers, cut into thin strips**
- **1 small red or white onion, thinly sliced and separated into rings**
- **½ cup vinegar**
- **¼ cup olive oil**
- **1 tablespoon sugar or sugar substitute* equivalent to 1 tablespoon sugar**
- **2 teaspoons snipped fresh tarragon or thyme or ½ teaspoon dried tarragon or thyme, crushed**
- **½ teaspoon ground black pepper**
- **Lettuce leaves (optional)**

1. In a covered large saucepan, cook fresh green beans and/or wax beans in a small amount of boiling water for 8 to 10 minutes or just until tender. (If using frozen beans, cook according to package directions, except omit the salt.) Drain beans in a colander, then submerge beans in ice water to cool quickly. Drain beans again. In a large bowl, combine cooked beans, canned beans, pepper strips, and onion rings.

2. For marinade, in a bowl, whisk together vinegar, olive oil, sugar, tarragon, and black pepper until combined. Pour marinade over bean mixture; toss gently to coat. Cover; chill for 4 to 24 hours, stirring occasionally.

3. To serve, line a serving bowl with lettuce leaves, if desired. Using a slotted spoon, spoon the bean salad into the bowl. Makes 14 (about ⅔-cup) servings.

***Sugar Substitutes:** Choose from Splenda granular, Equal Spoonful or packets, or Sweet'N Low bulk or packets. Follow the package directions to use product amount equivalent to 1 tablespoon sugar.

Grilled Herb Corn on the Cob

Grilled Herb Corn on the Cob

The corn steams in its own husks on the grill. How easy is that?

PER SERVING: 87 cal., 3 g total fat (0 g sat. fat), 0 mg chol., 109 mg sodium, 15 g carb., 2 g fiber, 3 g pro. Exchanges: 1 starch, 0.5 fat. Carb choices: 1.

- **6 fresh ears of corn**
- **2 tablespoons snipped fresh oregano or 2 teaspoons dried oregano, crushed**
- **2 tablespoons snipped fresh thyme or 2 teaspoons dried thyme, crushed**
- **1 tablespoon snipped fresh tarragon or 1 teaspoon dried tarragon, crushed**
- **2 tablespoons olive oil**
- **½ teaspoon salt**
- **¼ teaspoon ground black pepper**

1. Peel back corn husks but do not remove. Discard silks. Soak in cold water for 15 minutes; pat dry.

2. In a small bowl, combine oregano, thyme, and tarragon; set aside. In another small bowl, combine oil, salt, and pepper.

3. Brush corn with oil mixture. Sprinkle with herb mixture. Fold husks back around cobs. Tie with 100-percent-cotton kitchen string.

4. Place corn in a grill basket or directly on grill rack over medium coals. Grill for 25 to 30 minutes or until tender, turning and rearranging a few times during grilling. To serve, cut each ear of corn in half crosswise. Makes 12 servings.

Mixed Garden Greens Salad

Use your own favorite purchased salad blend, if you like.

PER SERVING: 99 cal., 7 g total fat (2 g sat. fat), 4 mg chol., 72 mg sodium, 7 g carb., 2 g fiber, 2 g pro. Exchanges: 1.5 vegetable, 1.5 fat. Carb choices: 0.5.

- **2 cups torn romaine**
- **2 cups torn fresh spinach**
- **1½ cups torn curly endive**
- **1½ cups arugula**
- **2 small red, green, and/or yellow sweet peppers, cut into thin strips**
- **1 small red onion, thinly sliced**
- **1 cup red or yellow grape, pear, or cherry tomatoes, halved**
- **1 medium carrot**
- **¼ cup finely shredded cheddar cheese (1 ounce)**
- **½ cup Low-Calorie French Salad Dressing (see recipe, below) or ½ cup bottled reduced-calorie French salad dressing**

1. In a large bowl, combine romaine, spinach, curly endive, arugula, sweet peppers, red onion, and tomatoes. Using a vegetable peeler, slice carrot lengthwise into long, thin ribbons. Top salad with carrot ribbons and cheddar cheese. Serve with Low-Calorie French Salad Dressing. Makes 8 (about 1-cup) servings.

Low-Calorie French Salad Dressing: In a blender, combine ¼ cup low-sodium tomato juice or vegetable juice, 3 tablespoons vinegar, 1 tablespoon honey, 1 teaspoon paprika, 1 minced garlic clove, 1 teaspoon Worcestershire sauce, ¼ teaspoon ground black pepper, and ⅛ teaspoon salt. With the blender running, slowly add ⅓ cup olive oil through the hole in the lid; continue blending until mixture reaches desired consistency. Cover and chill for up to 1 week. Makes about ¾ cup.

Grapefruit and Avocado Salad

Grapefruit and Avocado Salad

Splash the versatile orange salad dressing onto just about any combination of tossed salad ingredients.

PER SERVING: 106 cal., 7 g total fat (1 g sat. fat), 0 mg chol., 122 mg sodium, 11 g carb., 4 g fiber, 2 g pro. Exchanges: 1 vegetable, 0.5 fruit, 1 fat. Carb choices: 1.

4 cups packaged fresh baby spinach
1 grapefruit, peeled and sectioned
1 small avocado, halved, seeded, peeled, and sliced
1 cup canned sliced beets
1 tablespoon sliced almonds, toasted
1 recipe Orange Vinaigrette (see recipe, below)

1. Top spinach with grapefruit, avocado, beets, and almonds. Drizzle with Orange Vinaigrette. Makes 6 (about 1-cup) servings.

Orange Vinaigrette: In a screw-top jar, combine 1 teaspoon finely shredded orange peel, ⅓ cup orange juice, 2 teaspoons red wine vinegar, 2 teaspoons salad oil, ⅛ teaspoon salt, and a dash ground black pepper. Cover and shake well to mix.

Fresh Fruit Salad with Creamy Lime Topping

You can serve the lime-kissed cream over any mixed fruit for dessert, a salad, or a breakfast eye-opener.

PER SERVING: 64 cal., 1 g total fat (1 g sat. fat), 3 mg chol., 61 mg sodium, 13 g carb., 2 g fiber, 1 g pro. Exchanges: 1 fruit. Carb choices: 1.

½ cup light dairy sour cream
⅓ cup fat-free or light mayonnaise or salad dressing
1 teaspoon finely shredded lime peel
2 tablespoons powdered sugar
2 tablespoons lime juice
1 tablespoon fat-free milk (optional)
6 cups assorted fresh fruit (such as clementine segments, cut-up mango, raspberries, star fruit slices, pineapple chunks, cut-up kiwifruit, and/or halved strawberries)
Finely shredded lime peel (optional)

1. In a small bowl, stir together sour cream, mayonnaise, the 1 teaspoon lime peel, powdered sugar, and lime juice. If desired, stir in milk to make topping desired consistency.

2. To serve, spoon sour cream mixture onto fruit. If desired, garnish with additional lime peel. Makes 12 (½-cup) servings.

Make-Ahead Directions: Cover and chill sour cream mixture for up to 5 days.

Minty Melon Cups

Midori is a liqueur from Japan that's a vivid green with a flavor reminiscent of honeydew melon.

PER SERVING: 87 cal., 0 g total fat, 0 mg chol., 20 mg sodium, 18 g carb., 1 g fiber, 1 g pro. Exchanges: 1 fruit. Carb choices: 1.

10 cups cut-up melon or melon balls (such as watermelon, honeydew, canary melon, and/or cantaloupe)
½ cup Midori, other melon-flavor liqueur, or low-calorie ginger ale
2 tablespoons snipped fresh mint or 2 teaspoons dried mint, crushed

1. In a very large bowl, combine melon balls, Midori, and mint; toss gently to coat. Makes 10 (1-cup) servings.

Make-Ahead Directions: Cut up and store melon in covered containers in the refrigerator for up to 24 hours. Add liquid before serving.

Quick Tip:

Fruit salads such as the one pictured here make a perfect afternoon snack. Keep the Creamy Lime Topping ready in the refrigerator for when you crave something sweet. You can serve it over cut-up fruit or use it as a dipper for strawberries or pineapple chunks.

Fresh Fruit Salad with Creamy Lime Topping

eye-opening breakfasts

Bacon 'n' Egg Pockets

Breakfast is a must for both on-the-go weekdays and kick-back weekends. You can stir up some of our recipes the night before and bake in the morning. Others take just a few minutes to prepare. They all give your day a healthful, delicious start.

Bacon 'n' Egg Pockets

Creamy scrambled eggs and Canadian bacon pack these pita breads with protein. It's the perfect breakfast to eat at home or on the go.

PER SERVING: 162 cal., 4 g total fat (1 g sat. fat), 118 mg chol., 616 mg sodium, 18 g carb., 2 g fiber, 13 g pro. Exchanges: 1 starch, 1.5 very lean meat, 0.5 fat. Carb choices: 1.

2 eggs
4 egg whites
3 ounces Canadian-style bacon, chopped
3 tablespoons water
2 tablespoons sliced green onion (optional)
1/8 teaspoon salt
Nonstick cooking spray
2 large whole wheat pita bread rounds, halved crosswise

1. In a medium bowl, combine eggs, egg whites, Canadian bacon, the water, green onion (if using), and salt. Beat with a wire whisk until mixed.

2. Coat an unheated large nonstick skillet with cooking spray. Preheat over medium heat.

3. Add egg mixture to skillet. Cook, without stirring, until mixture begins to set on the bottom and around the edge. Using a large spatula, lift and fold the partially cooked egg mixture so the uncooked portion flows underneath. Continue cooking about 2 minutes or until the egg mixture is set but still glossy and moist. Remove from heat.

4. To serve, fill pita halves with egg mixture. Makes 4 servings.

Breakfast Pizza

A purchased Italian bread shell makes a perfect base for an Italian-style topper.

PER SERVING: 233 cal., 7 g total fat (2 g sat. fat), 11 mg chol., 579 mg sodium, 29 g carb., 2 g fiber, 15 g pro. Exchanges: 2 starch, 1.5 lean meat. Carb choices: 2.

Nonstick cooking spray
1½ cups loose-pack frozen diced hash brown potatoes with onions and peppers
1 clove garlic, minced
1½ cups refrigerated or frozen egg product, thawed
⅓ cup fat-free milk
1 tablespoon snipped fresh basil
½ teaspoon salt
¼ teaspoon ground black pepper
1 tablespoon olive oil
1 14-ounce Italian bread shell (such as Boboli brand)
1 cup shredded part-skim mozzarella cheese (4 ounces)
2 plum tomatoes, halved lengthwise and sliced
¼ cup shredded fresh basil and/or fresh basil leaves

1. Preheat oven to 375°F. Coat an unheated large nonstick skillet with cooking spray. Preheat over medium heat. Add potatoes and garlic. Cook and stir about 4 minutes or until the vegetables are tender.

2. Meanwhile, in a small bowl, stir together egg, milk, the 1 tablespoon snipped basil, salt, and pepper.

3. Add oil to potato mixture in skillet; add egg mixture. Cook, without stirring, until mixture begins to set on the bottom and around the edge. Using a large spatula, lift and fold partially cooked egg mixture so uncooked portion flows underneath. Continue cooking about 2 minutes or until egg is set but still glossy and moist. Remove from heat.

4. To assemble, place bread shell on a large baking sheet or 12-inch pizza pan. Top with half of the shredded mozzarella cheese, the cooked egg mixture, the tomatoes, and the remaining cheese.

5. Bake about 10 minutes or until cheese is melted. Sprinkle with the ¼ cup shredded basil and/or basil leaves. Cut pizza into wedges. Makes 8 servings.

Scrambled Eggs with Tomatoes and Peppers

Scrambled Eggs with Tomatoes and Peppers

Egg product and fat-free milk keep the fat content low.

PER SERVING: 114 cal., 4 g total fat (1 g sat. fat), 0 mg chol., 386 mg sodium, 7 g carb., 1 g fiber, 13 g pro. Exchanges: 2 lean meat, 0.5 vegetable, 1 fat. Carb choices: 0.5.

1 tablespoon olive oil
½ cup chopped onion
½ cup chopped red or green sweet pepper
½ cup chopped, seeded tomato
2 cups refrigerated or frozen egg product, thawed, or 8 eggs
⅓ cup fat-free milk
¼ teaspoon salt
⅛ teaspoon ground black pepper

1. In a large skillet, heat olive oil over medium heat. Add onion and sweet pepper; cook for 4 to 6 minutes or until tender, stirring occasionally. Stir in tomato.

2. Meanwhile, in a medium bowl, beat together eggs, milk, salt, and black pepper. Add egg mixture to onion mixture in skillet. Cook over medium heat, without stirring, until mixture begins to set on the bottom and around the edge.

3. With a spatula or a large spoon, gently lift and fold the partially cooked egg mixture so any uncooked egg portion flows underneath. Continue cooking over medium heat for 2 to 3 minutes or until the egg mixture is cooked through but still glossy and moist. Remove from heat. Serve warm. Makes 4 servings.

(egg substitutes)

Many recipes that call for eggs require the binding property found in the egg white. The white, primarily protein and water, is the main ingredient in most egg substitutes, or egg product. The yolk is omitted, along with most of the fat and cholesterol. Egg product can be used in many recipes that call for whole eggs. Or prepare your own substitute by using 2 egg whites for each whole egg called for in a recipe.

Breakfast Pizza

Vegetable Frittata
Flaxseed Banana Muffins (page 112)

Quick Tip:

Egg substitutes are great to keep on hand and use for many recipes. But sometimes you might only have eggs in the shell. When a recipe calls for several eggs or it needs a little richness or color, use 2 egg whites and 1 whole egg for every 2 eggs.

Vegetable Frittata

The frittata is a versatile dish. Add any vegetable-and-cheese combination that appeals to you.

PER SERVING: 141 cal., 8 g total fat (2 g sat. fat), 165 mg chol., 353 mg sodium, 5 g carb., 1 g fiber, 13 g pro. Exchanges: 0.5 vegetable, 2 lean meat, 0.5 fat. Carb choices: 0.

- **2 teaspoons olive oil**
- **½ cup coarsely chopped broccoli florets**
- **½ cup sliced fresh mushrooms**
- **½ cup chopped carrot**
- **¼ cup chopped onion**
- **6 egg whites***
- **3 eggs***
- **2 tablespoons snipped fresh basil**
- **¼ teaspoon salt**
- **¼ teaspoon ground black pepper**
- **⅓ cup shredded part-skim mozzarella cheese**

1. Preheat broiler. In a medium broilerproof skillet, heat oil over medium heat. Add broccoli, mushrooms, carrot, and onion; cook for 7 to 8 minutes or until vegetables are crisp-tender, stirring occasionally. (If vegetables start to overbrown, reduce heat.)

2. Meanwhile, in a medium bowl, whisk together egg whites, eggs, basil, salt, and pepper. Pour egg mixture onto vegetables in skillet. Cook over medium heat.

3. As mixture sets, run a spatula around the edge of the skillet, lifting the egg mixture so the uncooked portion flows underneath. Continue cooking and lifting edge until the egg mixture is almost set and the surface is just slightly moist.

4. Sprinkle cheese onto egg mixture. Broil 4 inches from the heat about 2 minutes or until the top is light brown and the center is set. Let stand for 5 minutes before serving. Makes 4 servings.

***Test Kitchen Tip:** If you like, you can substitute 1½ cups refrigerated or thawed frozen egg product for the egg whites and eggs.

Spinach and Cheese Omelet

Spinach and Cheese Omelet

A high-quality sharp cheddar adds the most flavor in the smallest quantity—and the fewest calories.

PER SERVING: 120 cal., 3 g total fat (2 g sat. fat), 10 mg chol., 438 mg sodium, 5 g carb., 1 g fiber, 16 g pro. Exchanges: 0.5 vegetable, 2 very lean meat, 0.5 fat. Carb choices: 0.

- **Nonstick cooking spray**
- **2 cups refrigerated or frozen egg product, thawed, or 8 eggs**
- **2 tablespoons snipped fresh chives, Italian (flat-leaf) parsley, or chervil**
- **⅛ teaspoon salt**
- **⅛ teaspoon cayenne pepper**
- **½ cup shredded reduced-fat sharp cheddar cheese**
- **2 cups fresh baby spinach leaves or torn fresh spinach**
- **1 recipe Red Pepper Relish (see recipe, below)**

1. Lightly coat a 10-inch nonstick skillet with a flared side with cooking spray. Heat skillet over medium-high heat.

2. In a bowl, whisk together eggs, chives, salt, and cayenne pepper until frothy. Pour mixture into hot skillet. Immediately begin stirring eggs gently but continuously with a wooden spatula until mixture resembles small pieces of cooked egg surrounded by liquid. Discontinue stirring; cook for 30 to 60 seconds more or until egg is set but shiny. Sprinkle with cheese. Top with spinach and half of Red Pepper Relish. With a spatula, lift and fold one side of omelet over filling. Transfer to a warm platter. Top with remaining relish. Makes 4 servings.

Red Pepper Relish: In a small bowl, stir together ⅔ cup chopped red sweet pepper, 2 tablespoons finely chopped onion, 1 tablespoon cider vinegar, and ¼ teaspoon ground black pepper. Makes ¾ cup.

Raisin-Carrot Muffins

Raisin-Carrot Muffins

Wheat germ and carrots up the fiber in these cakelike muffins. Buttermilk keeps them low in fat.

PER MUFFIN: 146 cal., 4 g total fat (1 g sat. fat), 14 mg chol., 168 mg sodium, 24 g carb., 2 g fiber, 4 g pro. Exchanges: 1 starch, 0.5 other carb., 0.5 fat. Carb choices: 1.5.

PER MUFFIN WITH SUBSTITUTE: same as above, except 127 cal., 19 g carb. Carb choices: 1.

2⁄3 cup golden raisins or dried currants
1⁄2 cup boiling water
Nonstick cooking spray
1 1⁄2 cups all-purpose flour
1⁄2 cup whole wheat flour
1⁄3 cup toasted wheat germ
1 1⁄2 teaspoons baking powder
1⁄2 teaspoon baking soda
1⁄2 teaspoon salt
1⁄2 teaspoon ground cinnamon
1 egg
1 1⁄4 cups buttermilk
1⁄3 cup packed brown sugar or brown sugar substitute* equivalent to 1⁄3 cup brown sugar
1⁄4 cup cooking oil
1 cup finely shredded carrots
Ground cinnamon

1. Preheat oven to 400°F. In a small bowl, combine raisins and boiling water; set aside. Coat sixteen 2 1⁄2-inch muffin cups with cooking spray or line with paper bake cups; set aside.

2. In a medium bowl, stir together all-purpose flour, whole wheat flour, wheat germ, baking powder, baking soda, salt, and the 1⁄2 teaspoon cinnamon. Make a well in the center.

3. In a small bowl, beat egg slightly; stir in buttermilk, brown sugar, and oil. Add all at once to flour mixture; stir just until moistened (the batter should be lumpy). Drain raisins. Gently fold raisins and carrots into batter. Spoon batter evenly into prepared muffin cups, filling each cup two-thirds full. Sprinkle tops with additional cinnamon.

4. Bake for 18 to 20 minutes or until golden. Cool in muffin cups on a wire rack for 5 minutes. Remove from cups. Serve warm. Makes 16 muffins.

***Sugar Substitutes:** Choose from Sweet'N Low Brown or Sugar Twin Granulated Brown. Follow package directions to use product amount equivalent to 1⁄3 cup brown sugar.

Flaxseed Banana Muffins

With four grains, each muffin boasts 4 grams of heart-healthy fiber.

PER MUFFIN: 161 cal., 8 g total fat (1 g sat. fat), 18 mg chol., 117 mg sodium, 19 g carb., 4 g fiber, 6 g pro. Exchanges: 1.5 starch, 1.5 fat. Carb choices: 1.

PER MUFFIN WITH SUBSTITUTE: same as above, except 140 cal., 15 g carb. Exchanges: 1 starch. Carb choices: 1.

Nonstick cooking spray
3⁄4 cup whole wheat flour
1⁄4 cup gluten flour (wheat gluten)
1⁄4 cup barley flour
1⁄4 cup oat bran
2 tablespoons wheat bran
1 teaspoon baking powder
1⁄4 teaspoon baking soda
1⁄4 teaspoon salt
1 egg or 1⁄4 cup refrigerated or frozen egg product, thawed
1 large very ripe banana, mashed (3⁄4 cup)
1⁄2 cup buttermilk or sour milk*
1⁄3 cup sugar or sugar substitute equivalent to 1⁄3 cup sugar**

¼ cup cooking oil
1 teaspoon vanilla
⅓ cup flaxseeds
¼ cup chopped walnuts (optional)

1. Preheat oven to 400°F. Coat twelve 2½-inch muffin cups with nonstick cooking spray, or line with paper bake cups and coat insides of paper cups with nonstick cooking spray; set aside.

2. In a medium bowl, combine whole wheat flour, gluten flour, barley flour, oat bran, wheat bran, baking powder, baking soda, and salt. Make a well in the center; set aside.

3. In another medium bowl, beat egg with a whisk; whisk in mashed banana, buttermilk, sugar, oil, and vanilla. Add egg mixture all at once to flour mixture. Stir just until moistened (the batter should be lumpy). Stir in flaxseeds and, if desired, walnuts.

4. Spoon batter into prepared muffin cups, filling each cup two-thirds full.

5. Bake about 15 minutes or until a toothpick inserted in centers comes out clean. Cool in muffin cups on a wire rack for 5 minutes. Remove from cups. Serve warm. Makes 12 muffins.

***Test Kitchen Tip:** To make ½ cup sour milk, place 1½ teaspoons lemon juice or vinegar in a glass measuring cup. Add enough fat-free milk to make ½ cup total liquid; stir. Let stand for 5 minutes.

****Sugar Substitutes:** Choose from Splenda granular, Equal Spoonful or packets, or Sweet'N Low bulk or packets. Follow directions to use amount equivalent to ⅓ cup sugar.

Blueberry-Oat Scones with Flaxseeds

Flaxseeds provide all eight essential amino acids and many nutrients, including omega-3 essential fatty acids. The tiny seeds may help lower cholesterol and blood glucose levels.

PER SCONE: 148 cal., 5 g total fat (3 g sat. fat), 10 mg chol., 133 mg sodium, 22 g carb., 2 g fiber, 4 g pro. Exchanges: 1.5 starch, 1 fat. Carb choices: 1.5.
PER SCONE WITH SUBSTITUTE: same as above, except 133 cal., 19 g carb. Exchanges: 1 starch. Carb choices: 1.

2 tablespoons flaxseeds, toasted
1½ cups all-purpose flour
½ cup rolled oats
¼ cup sugar or sugar substitute equivalent to ¼ cup sugar**
2 teaspoons baking powder
¼ teaspoon salt
¼ cup cold butter, cut into pieces
1 egg white
1 6-ounce carton plain fat-free or low-fat yogurt
1¼ cups fresh blueberries
Fat-free milk
Rolled oats and/or flaxseeds (optional)

1. Preheat oven to 400°F. Line a baking sheet with foil; set aside. Place the 2 tablespoons flaxseeds in a spice grinder; pulse until ground to a fine powder.

2. In a bowl, combine ground flaxseeds, flour, the ½ cup oats, the sugar, baking powder, and salt. Using a pastry blender, cut in butter until mixture resembles coarse crumbs. Make a well in the center of flour mixture; set aside. In a bowl, slightly beat egg white; stir in yogurt. Gently fold in berries. Add berry mixture all at once to flour mixture. With a fork, stir just until moistened.

3. Turn out dough onto a lightly floured surface. Knead by folding and gently pressing dough for 10 to 12 strokes or until nearly smooth. Pat or lightly roll dough into a 10-inch circle. Cut into 12 wedges; place 1 inch apart on baking sheet. Brush wedges with milk. If desired, sprinkle with oats and/or flaxseeds. Bake for 16 to 18 minutes or until golden. Serve warm. Makes 12 scones.

****Sugar Substitutes:** Choose from Splenda granular, Equal Spoonful or packets, or Sweet'N Low bulk or packets. Follow the package directions to use the product amount equivalent to ¼ cup sugar.

Blueberry-Oat Scones with Flaxseeds

Good Morning Cereal Blend

Top this fiber-filled cereal blend with fat-free milk or yogurt for a satisfying breakfast.

PER SERVING: 196 cal., 2 g total fat (0 g sat. fat), 0 mg chol., 140 mg sodium, 46 g carb., 8 g fiber, 6 g pro. Exchanges: 3 starch. Carb choices: 3.

8 cups whole-bran cereal
6 cups low-fat granola
4 cups wheat-and-barley nugget cereal (such as Grape Nuts cereal)
7 cups seven-grain-and-sesame cereal (such as Kashi Medley cereal)
2 cups dried cranberries and/or raisins

1. Combine cereals and cranberries. Cover and store cereal blend in airtight container for up to 2 weeks. Or seal in freezer bags; freeze for up to 3 months. Makes about 36 (3/4-cup) servings.

Honey-Apple Pancakes

These pancakes are like breakfast apple pies.

PER 2 PANCAKES: 122 cal., 3 g total fat (0 g sat. fat), 26 mg chol., 163 mg sodium, 22 g carb., 1 g fiber, 3 g pro. Exchanges: 0.5 starch. Carb choices: 1.5.

1¼ cups all-purpose flour
2 teaspoons baking powder
¼ teaspoon apple pie spice
⅛ teaspoon baking soda
1 beaten egg
¾ cup apple juice
2 tablespoons honey
1 tablespoon cooking oil
Nonstick cooking spray
Light or sugar-free pancake syrup (optional)

1. In a medium bowl, stir together flour, baking powder, 1/4 teaspoon *salt,* apple pie spice, and baking soda. Make a well in the center; set aside. In a bowl, stir together egg, apple juice, honey, and oil. Add egg mixture all at once to flour mixture; stir just until combined.

2. Lightly coat a heavy nonstick skillet with cooking spray. Heat over medium heat. For each pancake, pour 1/4 cup of batter onto hot skillet spreading to a 4-inch diameter. Cook for 2 to 3 minutes or until pancakes have bubbly surfaces and edges are slightly dry. Turn; cook for 2 to 3 minutes more or until golden brown. If desired, serve with syrup. Makes eight 4-inch pancakes.

Papaya-Strawberry Soymilk Smoothie

Try mango-blueberry, banana-grape, or other duets.

PER SERVING: 97 cal., 1 g total fat (0 g sat. fat), 0 mg chol., 47 mg sodium, 18 g carb., 2 g fiber, 3 g pro. Exchanges: 0.5 milk, 1 fruit. Carb choices: 1.

1 cup vanilla-flavored soymilk
½ cup orange juice
1 cup chopped papaya
½ cup frozen unsweetened whole strawberries
2 tablespoons soy protein powder (optional)
1 tablespoon honey (optional)

1. In a blender, combine soymilk, orange juice, fruit, and, if desired, protein powder and honey. Cover and blend until mixture is smooth. Immediately pour into three glasses. Makes about 3 (1-cup) servings.

(high fiber)

Fiber is important in helping regulate blood glucose levels. And you need lots of it—about 35 grams a day. Why all the fiber? It helps you eat less, lose weight, and feel better. Fiber fills you up without filling you out, keeps your digestive system regulated, and helps lower your body's level of the "bad" cholesterol—LDL cholesterol. The best sources are whole grains, fruits, and vegetables. Include whole grain cereals, breads, and pastas and beans and legumes in your meal plans. If you're not used to eating a high-fiber diet, remember to gradually increase your intake of fiber-rich foods and to drink lots of water.

Lemon Breakfast Parfaits

Lemon Breakfast Parfaits

Serve these lively layers of fruit and couscous for a smart start in the morning.

PER SERVING: 147 cal., 3 g total fat (1 g sat. fat), 7 mg chol., 61 mg sodium, 28 g carb., 4 g fiber, 5 g pro. Exchanges: 0.5 fruit, 1 starch, 0.5 fat. Carb choices: 2.

¾ cup fat-free milk
Dash salt
⅓ cup whole what or regular couscous
½ cup lemon low-fat yogurt
½ cup light dairy sour cream
1 tablespoon honey
¼ teaspoon finely shredded lemon peel
3 cups assorted fresh fruit, such as sliced strawberries, kiwifruit, nectarine, or star fruit, and/or blueberries, or raspberries
Chopped crystallized ginger (optional)
Fresh mint (optional)

1. In a medium saucepan, bring milk and salt to boiling; stir in couscous. Simmer, covered, for 1 minute. Remove from heat; let stand for 5 minutes. Stir with a fork until fluffy. Cool.

2. In a small bowl, combine yogurt, sour cream, honey, and lemon peel; stir into couscous. In another bowl, combine desired fruit.

3. To serve, divide half of the fruit mixture among six parfait glasses. Spoon couscous mixture over fruit; top with remaining fruit. If desired, garnish with chopped crystallized ginger and mint. Makes 6 servings.

good-for-you snacks

Citrus Salsa with Baked Chips

Healthful, homemade snacks help to keep your blood glucose levels in check. It's easy to make your own nibbles and dips to have on hand at home. At work, stash some quick-prep energy bars in your desk to avoid trips to the vending machine for high-fat chips or salt-laden pretzels.

Citrus Salsa with Baked Chips

Oranges and grapefruit meet tomatoes.

PER SERVING: 44 cal., 0 g total fat, 0 mg chol., 80 mg sodium, 10 g carb., 2 g fiber, 1 g pro. Exchanges: 0.5 starch. Carb choices: 0.5.

4 corn tortillas
Nonstick cooking spray
½ cup chopped grapefruit segments*
½ cup chopped orange segments*
½ cup chopped tomato
½ cup chopped cucumber
2 tablespoons chopped green onion
2 tablespoons snipped fresh cilantro
¼ teaspoon salt
¼ teaspoon crushed red pepper

1. Preheat oven to 400°F. For chips, lightly coat one side of each tortilla with cooking spray. Cut tortillas into 8 wedges. Arrange on an ungreased baking sheet. Bake for 8 to 10 minutes or until light brown and crisp. Cool.

2. For salsa, in a small bowl, stir together grapefruit segments, orange segments, tomato, cucumber, green onion, cilantro, salt, and red pepper. Makes 8 servings (¼ cup salsa and 4 chips each).

Make-Ahead Directions: Prepare chips as directed in Step 1. Place in an airtight container; cover and store at room temperature for up to 3 days. Prepare salsa as directed in Step 2. Spoon into an airtight container; cover and store in refrigerator for up to 4 hours.

***Test Kitchen Tip:** You can substitute other varieties of citrus fruits (such as clementines, blood oranges, cara cara oranges, kumquats, and/or tangerines) for the grapefruit and/or oranges.

Quick Tip:

Purchased chips and snack foods are generally high in both fat and calories. Making your own snacks keeps your health goals in check. Because you make them yourself, you have control over what is added. Your prep time is worth the health benefits.

Chutney-Topped Cheese Rounds

Light semisoft cheese helps keep these low in carbs, fat, and calories.

PER SERVING: 68 cal., 3 g total fat (2 g sat. fat), 15 mg chol., 160 mg sodium, 5 g carb., 1 g fiber, 6 g pro. Exchanges: 1 lean meat. Carb choices: 0.

½ cup finely chopped fresh peach or frozen unsweetened peach slices, thawed
1 tablespoon finely chopped dried cherries
1 teaspoon lemon juice
⅛ teaspoon ground cinnamon
4 0.75-ounce rounds light semisoft cheese

1. For chutney, in a bowl, combine peach, cherries, lemon juice, and cinnamon. Toss gently to combine.

2. To serve, split each cheese round in half horizontally. Spoon peach mixture onto the half-rounds. If desired, arrange half-rounds in a circle on a microwave-safe plate; microwave on 100 percent power (high) for 20 to 35 seconds or just until cheese is softened. Makes 4 (2-half-round) servings.

Make-Ahead Directions: Prepare as in Step 1. Cover and chill for up to 6 hours. Continue as in Step 2.

Crispy Parmesan Chips

These light-as-air chips are great on their own or used as dippers (see pages 124 and 125 for dip recipes).

PER 10 CHIPS: 103 cal., 4 g total fat (1 g sat. fat), 4 mg chol., 168 mg sodium, 14 g carb., 0 g fiber, 3 g pro. Exchanges: 1 starch, 0.5 fat. Carb choices: 1.

30 wonton wrappers
Nonstick cooking spray
2 tablespoons olive oil
1 clove garlic, minced
½ teaspoon dried basil, crushed
¼ cup grated Parmesan cheese or Romano cheese

1. Preheat oven to 350°F. Using a sharp knife, cut wonton wrappers diagonally in half to form 60 triangles. Coat a baking sheet with cooking spray. Arrange a third of the triangles in a single layer on baking sheet.

2. Stir together oil, garlic, and basil. Lightly brush wonton triangles with some of the oil mixture; sprinkle with cheese. Bake about 8 minutes or until golden. Cool completely. Repeat with remaining wonton triangles, oil mixture, and cheese. Makes 60 chips.

Chutney-Topped Cheese Rounds

Crispy Parmesan Chips

(snack sense)

Snacking is important to any balanced diet. It helps your body go with the flow during the day and keeps your energy expenditure on an even keel, with fewer peaks and valleys. When you take the edge off of your appetite, you tend to eat less during mealtimes. Some of the best snacks to enjoy are those high in protein. Yogurt fits that role well. Keep some frozen fruit (such as strawberries or tart cherries) in the freezer and plain nonfat yogurt in the fridge. Thaw some fruit in the microwave, add some yogurt, and sweeten with your favorite sweetener. Toss in a few walnuts for crunch. Yum!

Peanut-Stuffed Belgian Endive

Basil-Garlic Tomatoes

Basil-Garlic Tomatoes

Try another herb such as oregano or thyme in these tiny red treats.

PER SERVING: 31 cal., 1 g total fat (1 g sat. fat), 4 mg chol., 27 mg sodium, 4 g carb., 1 g fiber, 2 g pro. Exchanges: 0.5 vegetable. Carb choices: 0.

2 tablespoons light dairy sour cream
2 tablespoons snipped fresh basil
1 tablespoon light cream cheese
1 clove garlic, minced
16 cherry tomatoes, halved

1. In a small bowl, combine sour cream, basil, cream cheese, and garlic. Stir until mixed. Place sour cream mixture in a resealable plastic bag; seal. Cut a small hole in one corner. Pipe onto cut sides of tomato halves. Makes 4 (8-tomato-half) servings.

Make-Ahead Directions: In bowl, stir ingredients to mix. Cover; chill for up to 24 hours before piping.

Peanut-Stuffed Belgian Endive

Coleslaw takes on a new dimension when tossed with hoisin sauce.

PER SERVING: 100 cal., 6 g total fat (1 g sat. fat), 0 mg chol., 158 mg sodium, 9 g carb., 2 g fiber, 4 g pro. Exchanges: 0.5 high-fat meat, 1 vegetable, 0.5 fat. Carb choices: 0.5.

2 tablespoons bottled hoisin sauce
2 teaspoons creamy peanut butter
1 teaspoon water
½ teaspoon cider vinegar
⅛ teaspoon crushed red pepper (optional)
2 cups packaged shredded cabbage with carrot (coleslaw mix)
¼ cup unsalted peanuts, chopped
16 green or red Belgian endive leaves or 4 butterhead (Bibb or Boston) lettuce leaves

1. In a small bowl, whisk together hoisin sauce, peanut butter, the water, vinegar, and, if desired, red pepper. Add coleslaw mix and nuts; toss to coat.

2. Spoon mixture into endive leaves or divide among lettuce leaves; roll up lettuce leaves, if using. Makes 4 servings (4 filled endive leaves or 1 lettuce wrap each).

Spinach-Turkey Roll-Ups

It's a wrap, but turkey instead of a tortilla keeps the carbs low.

PER SERVING: 40 cal., 1 g total fat (1 g sat. fat), 9 mg chol., 220 mg sodium, 2 g carb., 0 g fiber, 5 g pro. Exchanges: 1 very lean meat. Carb choices: 0.

2 teaspoons honey mustard
Dash ground nutmeg
8 thin slices oven-roasted turkey breast (3 ounces)
1 cup fresh baby spinach leaves or fresh basil leaves
½ of a medium red or green sweet pepper, seeded and cut into thin strips
4 sticks mozzarella string cheese, cut lengthwise into quarters

1. In a small bowl, stir together honey mustard and nutmeg. Carefully spread mustard mixture evenly onto turkey slices.

2. Divide spinach evenly and place on turkey slices, allowing leaves to extend beyond the turkey. Top with pepper strips and cheese.

3. Starting at an edge of a turkey slice with cheese, roll up each turkey slice. If desired, cut each roll-up in half. Makes 8 servings.

Make-Ahead Directions: Prepare turkey roll-ups as directed. Wrap each roll-up in plastic wrap. Chill roll-ups for up to 4 hours.

Hold-That-Lime Strawberries

Hold-That-Lime Strawberries

Four ingredients are all you need for this delicious dip.

PER SERVING: 58 cal., 0 g total fat, 2 mg chol., 36 mg sodium, 12 g carb., 2 g fiber, 1 g pro. Exchanges: 1 fruit. Carb choices: 1.

- **1 8-ounce carton fat-free dairy sour cream or light dairy sour cream**
- **2 tablespoons powdered sugar**
- **2 teaspoons finely shredded lime peel**
- **1 tablespoon lime juice**
- **4 cups fresh strawberries**

1. For dip, in a small storage container, stir together sour cream, powdered sugar, lime peel, and lime juice; cover and chill until serving time.

2. Wash strawberries, but do not remove stems or caps. Drain strawberries on paper towels. Transfer strawberries to a storage container; cover and chill until serving time.

3. Serve berries with dip. Makes 8 servings (2 tablespoons dip and ½ cup strawberries each).

Pesto and Tomato Bruschetta

Arugula adds a twist to the traditional Italian pine nut pesto.

PER SERVING: 92 cal., 5 g total fat (1 g sat. fat), 3 mg chol., 217 mg sodium, 9 g carb., 1 g fiber, 4 g pro. Exchanges: 0.5 starch, 1 fat. Carb choices: 0.5.

- **1 recipe Pine Nut Pesto (see recipe, below)**
- **24 ½-inch-thick slices baguette-style French bread, toasted, or whole grain crackers**
- **1 ounce Parmesan or Romano cheese, shaved**
- **1 cup red and/or yellow cherry tomatoes, halved or quartered, or 2 plum tomatoes, sliced**
- **Fresh basil sprigs (optional)**
- **Pine nuts, chopped walnuts, or chopped almonds, toasted (optional)**

1. Spread Pine Nut Pesto onto baguette slices. Top with shaved Parmesan and tomatoes. If desired, top with basil and nuts. Makes 12 (2-slice) servings.

Pine Nut Pesto: In a small food processor, combine 1 cup firmly packed fresh basil; 1 cup torn fresh arugula or spinach; ¼ cup grated Parmesan or Romano cheese; ¼ cup toasted pine nuts, chopped walnuts, or chopped almonds; 1 quartered clove garlic; 1 tablespoon olive oil; 1 tablespoon white balsamic vinegar; and ¼ teaspoon salt. Cover and process with several on-off turns until a paste forms, stopping several times to scrape the side. Process in enough water, adding 1 tablespoon at a time, until pesto reaches the consistency of soft butter.

Make-Ahead Directions: Toast bread slices and prepare Pine Nut Pesto as directed. Cover and chill for up to 24 hours. Serve as directed in Step 1.

Quick Tip:

Traditional pesto is delicious but can be high in fat and calories. When your basil is in abundance, why not make your own pesto? It will put any purchased pesto to shame. Keep it covered in the refrigerator for up to one week. Use it in omelets, on bread, or tossed with pasta.

Pesto and Tomato Bruschetta

White Bean Hummus

The chipotle pepper in adobo sauce lends a touch of heat and a smoky accent to this velvety dip.

PER SERVING: 57 cal., 1 g total fat (0 g sat. fat), 2 mg chol., 166 mg sodium, 9 g carb., 2 g fiber, 3 g pro. Exchanges: 0.5 vegetable, 0.5 starch. Carb choices: 0.5.

- **1 15-ounce can navy beans, rinsed and drained**
- **¼ cup light dairy sour cream**
- **2 tablespoons light mayonnaise**
- **1 tablespoon fat-free milk**
- **½ of a canned chipotle chile pepper in adobo sauce (optional)**
- **¼ teaspoon ground cumin**
- **1 clove garlic, chopped**
- **Snipped fresh chives (optional)**
- **Sliced cucumber**

1. In a food processor,* combine beans, sour cream, mayonnaise, milk, chipotle pepper (if desired), cumin, and garlic. Cover and process until smooth, scraping side of container as needed.

2. Transfer hummus to a serving bowl. If desired, sprinkle with chives. Serve with cucumber slices. Makes 12 servings (2 tablespoons hummus and 4 or 5 cucumber slices each).

***Test Kitchen Tip:** For a chunkier hummus, place beans in a medium bowl and mash with potato masher or fork until nearly smooth. Stir in remaining ingredients.

Roasted Red Pepper Dip

This creamy dip is perfect with celery sticks.

PER 2 TABLESPOONS DIP: 23 cal., 0 g total fat, 0 mg chol., 72 mg sodium, 4 g carb., 0 g fiber, 1 g pro. Exchanges: free. Carb choices: 0.

- **1 8-ounce carton fat-free dairy sour cream or light dairy sour cream**
- **¼ cup chopped bottled roasted red sweet peppers**
- **2 tablespoons sliced green onion**
- **1 tablespoon snipped fresh basil or ½ teaspoon dried basil, crushed**
- **1 clove garlic, minced**
- **¼ teaspoon salt**

1. In a small bowl, stir together sour cream, roasted red peppers, green onion, basil, garlic, and salt. Cover and chill for 4 to 24 hours to allow flavors to blend.

2. Stir dip before serving. Serve with assorted vegetable dippers, baked tortilla chips, and/or baked pita chips. Makes about 1¼ cups.

Creamy Peanut Dip

Use regular peanut butter because the reduced-fat kind has more carbs.

PER SERVING: 82 cal., 4 g total fat (1 g sat. fat), 0 mg chol., 42 mg sodium, 10 g carb., 2 g fiber, 2 g pro. Exchanges: 1 fat, 0.5 other carb. Carb choices: 0.5.

- **2 tablespoons creamy peanut butter**
- **1 tablespoon fat-free milk**
- **⅓ cup frozen fat-free whipped dessert topping, thawed**
- **Red and/or green pear or apple wedges***

1. In a small bowl, whisk together peanut butter and milk until combined. Gently fold in whipped dessert topping, leaving some streaks of whipped topping. Serve with fruit wedges. Makes 4 servings (2 tablespoons dip and 2 pear wedges each).

***Test Kitchen Tip:** To prevent cut fruit from browning, toss with a little orange or lemon juice.

(10 great snacks)

To avoid getting too hungry between meals, always carry a healthy, portable snack with you.

1. **Pair** plain yogurt with blueberries for a treat that has a similar texture to ice cream.
2. **Combine** a banana with almond butter. The combo keeps you satisfied for a longer time than either on its own because of the fiber in the banana and the protein and fat in the almond butter.
3. **Turn to** hummus with pita bread. Add some veggies to make a sandwich.
4. **Snack on** salsa and baked tortilla chips. Purchase the baked varieties to lower fat, and be sure to look for those that list zero trans fats on their nutrition labels.
5. **Nosh on** light microwave popcorn for its high fiber and B vitamin content.
6. **Top** low-fat chocolate pudding with low-fat granola.
7. **Stir** chopped peaches (packed in juice) into low-fat cottage cheese and sprinkle with sliced almonds.
8. **Stir together** some canned salmon, reduced-fat mayonnaise, and Cajun seasoning. Serve with whole grain crackers.
9. **Spread** apple slices with sunflower-seed butter.
10. **Spoon** some apple butter on a rice cake.

Lemon Avocado Dip

Use light sour cream; it's lower in carbs than fat-free sour cream.

PER SERVING: 72 cal., 5 g total fat (1 g sat. fat), 5 mg chol., 49 mg sodium, 7 g carb., 3 g fiber, 2 g pro. Exchanges: 1 vegetable, 1 fat. Carb choices: 0.5.

1 ripe avocado, halved, seeded, and peeled
1 tablespoon lemon juice or lime juice
½ cup light dairy sour cream
1 clove garlic, minced
⅛ teaspoon salt
Lemon wedge (optional)
4 medium red, yellow, and/or green sweet peppers, seeded and cut into strips

1. In a bowl, mash avocado with lemon juice. Stir in sour cream, garlic, and salt. If desired, garnish with lemon wedge. Serve with pepper strips. Makes 8 servings (2 tablespoons dip and ½ pepper each).

Make-Ahead Directions: Prepare as directed. Cover surface of dip with plastic wrap; chill for up to 4 hours.

Herbed Soy Snacks

Each serving of these roasted soybeans is rich in protein, polyunsaturated fats, and phytoestrogens. Enjoy these soynuts alone or mix with popcorn or other party mixes.

PER SERVING: 75 cal., 3 g total fat (1 g sat. fat), 0 mg chol., 17 mg sodium, 4 g carb., 3 g fiber, 7 g pro. Exchanges: 0.5 starch, 0.5 medium-fat meat. Carb choices: 0.

- **8 ounces dry roasted soybeans (2 cups)**
- **1½ teaspoons dried thyme, crushed**
- **¼ teaspoon garlic salt**
- **⅛ to ¼ teaspoon cayenne pepper**

1. Preheat oven to 350°F. In a 15×10×1-inch baking pan, spread soybeans in an even layer. In a small bowl, combine thyme, garlic salt, and cayenne pepper. Sprinkle soybeans with thyme mixture. Bake for 5 minutes or just until heated through, shaking pan once. Cool completely. Store up to 1 week at room temperature in an airtight container. Makes 16 (2-tablespoon) servings.

Sweet Chili Soy Snacks: Prepare Herbed Soy Snacks as directed, except increase garlic salt to ½ teaspoon and combine with 2 teaspoons brown sugar and 1½ teaspoons chili powder; sprinkle over soybeans before baking. Omit thyme and cayenne pepper.

Sesame-Ginger Soy Snacks: Prepare Herbed Soy Snacks as directed, except combine 2 teaspoons toasted sesame oil, ¾ teaspoon ground ginger, and ½ teaspoon onion salt; sprinkle over soybeans before baking. Omit thyme, garlic salt, and cayenne pepper.

Indian-Spiced Soy Snacks: Prepare Herbed Soy Snacks as directed, except combine ½ teaspoon garam masala and ¼ teaspoon salt with cayenne pepper; sprinkle over soybeans before baking. Omit thyme and garlic salt.

Oriental Trail Mix

Just four ingredients add up to a satisfying snack.

PER SERVING: 102 cal., 3 g total fat (1 sat. fat), 0 mg chol., 78 mg sodium, 17 g carb., 1 g fiber, 2 g pro. Exchanges: 1 starch, 0.5 fat. Carb choices: 1.

- **4 cups assorted oriental rice crackers**
- **¾ cup dried apricots, halved lengthwise**
- **¾ cup lightly salted cashews**
- **¼ cup crystallized ginger pieces and/or golden raisins**

1. In a medium bowl, stir together all ingredients. Serve immediately. Makes 16 (⅓-cup) servings.

Herbed Soy Snacks

Fruit and Peanut Snack Mix

This snack has a little of everything—the sweetness of the colorful dried fruit, the zest of the cheese-flavored crackers, and the satisfying crunch of peanuts.

PER SERVING: 212 cal., 8 g total fat (2 g sat. fat), 5 mg chol., 139 mg sodium, 34 g carb., 3 g fiber, 5 g pro. Exchanges: 1 fruit, 1.5 starch, 1 fat. Carb choices: 2.

- **1 6-ounce package plain, pretzel, and/or cheddar cheese-flavored bite-size fish-shape crackers (1½ cups)**
- **1 6-ounce package dried cranberries (1½ cups)**
- **1 7-ounce package dried pears, snipped (1⅓ cups)**
- **1 cup cocktail peanuts**

1. In a medium bowl, stir together all ingredients. Serve immediately. Makes about 12 (½-cup) servings.

Cherry-Almond Snack Mix

Herbed Mixed Nuts

This mix is good to have on hand when you need a snack to tide you over until mealtime.

PER SERVING: 199 cal., 16 g total fat (2 g sat. fat), 3 mg chol., 81 mg sodium, 8 g carb., 4 g fiber, 9 g pro. Exchanges: 0.5 starch, 1 high-fat meat, 1.5 fat. Carb choices: 0.5.

- **1 tablespoon butter, melted**
- **1 tablespoon Worcestershire sauce**
- **2 teaspoons dried basil and/or oregano, crushed**
- **½ teaspoon garlic salt**
- **3 cups walnuts, soy nuts, and/or almonds**
- **2 tablespoons grated Parmesan cheese**

1. Preheat oven to 325°F. In a bowl, combine melted butter, Worcestershire sauce, herb, and garlic salt. Add nuts; stir to coat.

2. Line a 15×10×1-inch baking pan with foil; spread nuts in pan. Top with Parmesan; stir to coat. Bake for 15 minutes, stirring twice. Cool. Cover tightly; store up to 1 week. Makes 12 (¼-cup) servings.

Cherry-Almond Snack Mix

Almonds star in this handy snack or breakfast cereal.

PER SERVING: 82 cal., 3 g total fat (1 g sat. fat), 3 mg chol., 58 mg sodium, 12 g carb., 1 g fiber, 2 g pro. Exchanges: 1 carb., 0.5 fat. Carb choices: 1.

- **4 cups sweetened oat square cereal**
- **½ cup sliced almonds**
- **2 tablespoons butter, melted**
- **½ teaspoon apple pie spice**
- **Dash salt**
- **1 cup dried cherries and/or golden raisins**

1. Preheat oven to 300°F. In a 15×10×1-inch baking pan, combine cereal and almonds. In a small bowl, stir together melted butter, apple pie spice, and salt. Drizzle butter mixture onto cereal mixture; toss to coat cereal and almonds evenly.

2. Bake about 20 minutes or until almonds are toasted, stirring once during baking. Cool snack mix in pan on a wire rack for 20 minutes.

3. Stir in cherries. Cool mixture completely. Cover tightly; store up to 1 week. Makes 20 (¼-cup) servings.

Chili Mixed Nuts

This will squelch your hungries, but be sure to watch your serving size. Nuts pack in calories that can add up fast.

PER SERVING: 232 cal., 21 g total fat (3 g sat. fat), 0 mg chol., 269 mg sodium, 8 g carb., 3 g fiber, 6 g pro. Exchanges: 0.5 starch, 1 high-fat meat, 2 fat. Carb choices: 0.5.

- **3 cups mixed nuts or peanuts**
- **1 tablespoon olive oil**
- **2 teaspoons chili powder**
- **½ teaspoon garlic powder**
- **½ teaspoon ground cumin**
- **¼ teaspoon cayenne pepper**
- **1¼ teaspoons celery salt**
- **¼ teaspoon ground cinnamon**

1. Preheat oven to 325°F. In a bowl, combine nuts and oil; stir to coat. In another bowl, stir together chili powder, garlic powder, cumin, cayenne pepper, celery salt, and cinnamon; sprinkle on nut mixture. Toss to coat.

2. Spread nuts in a 15×10×1-inch baking pan. Bake for 15 minutes, stirring twice. Cool. Cover tightly; store up to 2 weeks. Makes 12 (¼-cup) servings.

(nutty note)

Nuts are plucky little packets of nutrition power. True, a lot of calories are packed into each bite, but most of those calories come from heart-healthy monounsaturated fats that keep cholesterol in check. Besides providing energy, nuts contain important trace minerals, such as calcium, zinc, and the antioxidant mineral selenium. One of the best sources of vitamin E, nuts also are rich in folate and other B vitamins. Because of their high calorie content, limit your intake to only a few.

Spiced Popcorn

Spiced Popcorn

Zip up a bowl of popcorn with a few well-chosen spices.

PER SERVING: 31 cal., 0 g total fat, 0 mg chol., 50 mg sodium, 6 g carb., 1 g fiber, 1 g pro. Exchanges: 0.5 starch. Carb choices: 0.5.

½ teaspoon ground cumin
½ teaspoon chili powder
¼ to ½ teaspoon salt
Dash cayenne pepper
Dash ground cinnamon
12 cups air-popped popcorn
Nonstick cooking spray

1. In a small bowl, stir together cumin, chili powder, salt, cayenne pepper, and cinnamon; set aside.

2. Remove uncooked kernels from popped corn. Spread popcorn in a large shallow baking pan. Lightly coat popcorn with cooking spray. Sprinkle cumin mixture evenly over popcorn; toss gently to coat. Makes 12 (1-cup) servings.

Indian-Spiced Popcorn: Prepare Spiced Popcorn as directed, except substitute ½ teaspoon curry powder, ½ teaspoon garam masala, ¼ teaspoon ground turmeric, and ¼ teaspoon ground black pepper for the cumin, chili powder, cayenne pepper, and cinnamon.

Quick Tip:

If you thought energy bars were recent concoctions created for athletes, think again. Legend has it that medieval Italian crusaders toted a version called *panforte*—bread of strength—to sustain them on long journeys. Make your own for the best you can get.

Make-Your-Own Energy Bars

Modern-day crusaders on a quest for fitness can make their own fruit-and-nut bars for optimal health.

PER BAR: 126 cal., 3 g total fat (0 g sat. fat), 9 mg chol., 30 mg sodium, 24 g carb., 1 g fiber, 2 g pro. Exchanges: 1 fruit, 0.5 starch, 0.5 fat. Carb choices: 1.5.

Nonstick cooking spray
1 cup quick-cooking rolled oats
½ cup all-purpose flour
½ cup wheat-and-barley nugget cereal (such as Grape Nuts cereal)
½ to 1 teaspoon ground ginger
1 egg, beaten
⅓ cup unsweetened applesauce
3 tablespoons packed brown sugar
3 tablespoons honey
2 tablespoons cooking oil
2 7-ounce packages mixed dried fruit bits
¼ cup shelled sunflower seeds
¼ cup chopped walnuts

1. Preheat oven to 325°F. Line an 8×8×2-inch baking pan with foil. Coat foil with cooking spray. Set pan aside.

2. In a large bowl, combine oats, flour, cereal, and ginger. Add egg, applesauce, brown sugar, honey, and oil; mix well. Stir in fruit bits, sunflower seeds, and walnuts. Press mixture evenly into prepared pan.

3. Bake for 30 to 35 minutes or until lightly browned around the edges. Cool on a wire rack. Lift edges of foil to remove bars from pan; cut. Makes 24 bars.

Pick-Me-Up Energy Bars

Dates and whole wheat flour provide a combination of fast carb energy along with slower carb energy to help pick you up and keep you energized.

PER BAR: 89 cal., 1 g total fat (0 g sat. fat), 0 mg chol., 36 mg sodium, 20 g carb., 2 g fiber, 2 g pro. Exchanges: 1 fruit, 0.5 starch. Carb choices: 1.

Nonstick cooking spray
3 tablespoons honey
¼ cup orange juice
2 tablespoons lemon juice
24 pitted whole dates, snipped
2½ cups whole wheat flour
½ teaspoon baking soda
¼ teaspoon baking powder
¼ cup unsweetened applesauce
3 tablespoons pure maple syrup
2 egg whites
1 tablespoon canola or cooking oil

1. Preheat oven to 350°F. Line a 13×9×2-inch baking pan with foil. Lightly coat foil with cooking spray; set aside. In a small bowl, combine honey, orange juice, and lemon juice. Stir in the dates; set aside.

2. In a large mixing bowl, combine the flour, soda, and baking powder. In a second bowl, combine applesauce, syrup, egg whites, and oil. Add applesauce mixture to flour mixture. Beat with an electric mixer until just combined (mixture will be crumbly). Stir in date mixture. Spoon batter in the prepared baking pan; press evenly into pan with fingers or the back of the spoon.

3. Bake for 12 to 15 minutes or until a toothpick inserted near the center comes out clean. Cool on a wire rack. Lift edges of foil to remove bars from pan; cut. Makes 24 bars.

Test Kitchen Tip: To store, wrap and freeze individual bars. Thaw before eating.

Apricot Iced Tea

You'll need a gallon-size heatproof pitcher to brew the tea, or divide it between two 2-quart pitchers.

PER SERVING: 55 cal., 0 g total fat, 0 mg chol., 3 mg sodium, 14 g carb., 1 g fiber, 0 g pro. Exchanges: 1 fruit. Carb choices: 1.

16 black tea bags
12 cups boiling water
1 cup loosely packed fresh mint
6 12-ounce cans apricot nectar
2 teaspoons vanilla
Ice cubes
Fresh apricot wedges (optional)
Fresh mint sprigs (optional)

1. In a 1-gallon heatproof pitcher, combine tea bags, boiling water, and the 1 cup mint leaves. Let steep for 5 minutes.

2. Remove and discard tea bags and mint. Cover tea; let stand for 1 hour.

3. Stir apricot nectar and vanilla into tea; cover and chill until serving time.

4. To serve, fill tall glasses with ice cubes. Add tea. If desired, garnish with apricot wedges and/or mint sprigs. Makes 21 (8-ounce) servings.

Make-Ahead Directions: Prepare apricot tea mixture as directed through Step 3; cover and chill for up to 48 hours before serving as in Step 4.

Pomegranate Cooler

Kids love this fizzy fruit drink—a nutritious alternative to high-carb sodas.

PER SERVING: 38 cal., 0 g total fat, 0 mg chol., 7 mg sodium, 9 g carb., 0 g fiber, 0 g pro. Exchanges: 0.5 fruit. Carb choices: 0.5.

1 cup pomegranate juice (half of a 16-ounce bottle), chilled
½ cup chopped fresh pineapple
2 cups ice cubes
1 cup diet lemon-lime carbonated beverage, chilled

1. In a blender, combine juice and pineapple; cover and blend until smooth. Gradually add ice cubes, blending until slushy.

2. Transfer to a pitcher. Slowly pour in the carbonated beverage. Pour into glasses. Makes 5 (6-ounce) servings.

Chocolate-Banana Sipper

Chocolate-Banana Sipper

This midafternoon snack drink is simply superb. Halve the ingredients for a 2-serving sipper.

PER SERVING: 122 cal., 1 g total fat (0 g sat. fat), 2 mg chol., 65 mg sodium, 23 g carb., 1 g fiber, 5 g pro. Exchanges: 1 carb., 0.5 milk. Carb choices: 1.5.

2 cups fat-free milk
1 medium banana, sliced and frozen*
2 to 3 tablespoons unsweetened cocoa powder
2 tablespoons honey
1 teaspoon vanilla

1. In a blender, combine milk, banana, cocoa powder, honey, and vanilla. Cover and blend until smooth and frothy. Makes 4 (1-cup) servings.

***Test Kitchen Tip:** Peel and slice banana. Place banana slices in a single layer on a baking sheet lined with plastic wrap. Freeze at least 1 hour or until firm.

delightful desserts

Honey-Apricot Frozen Yogurt (back), page 134
Very Berry Sorbet (middle), opposite
Strawberry Sherbet (front), page 134

Rocky Road Parfaits

1. In a medium saucepan, stir together mango nectar and unflavored gelatin. Cook and stir over low heat until gelatin is dissolved. Remove from heat.

2. Stir in lime juice and, if using, food coloring. Cover and chill about 2 hours or until mixture mounds when lifted with a spoon, stirring occasionally.

3. Gently whisk whipped topping into mango mixture until smooth. Spoon into eight dessert dishes or parfait glasses. Cover; chill about 2 hours or until set.

4. Arrange mango strips on top of mango mixture. If desired, garnish each serving with a mint leaf. Makes 8 servings (1/3 cup mousse and fruit each).

Mango Mousse

Quick Tip:

Aspartame, one of the most popular sugar substitutes, isn't stable when heated and can't be used for cooking and baking, but acesulfame K is stable when heated. For all sugar alternatives, read the labels to be sure you'll get the sweet rewards you seek—with success.

Strawberry Sherbet

This luscious strawberry delight is made from packaged frozen strawberries. Be sure to use strawberries packed in light syrup. Pictured on *page 132*.

PER SERVING: 68 cal., 0 g total fat, 1 mg chol., 33 mg sodium, 14 g carb., 0 g fiber, 2 g pro. Exchanges: 1 carb. Carb choices: 1.

- **¼ cup sugar**
- **4 teaspoons cornstarch**
- **1 teaspoon finely shredded lemon peel**
- **1 12-ounce can evaporated fat-free milk**
- **1½ teaspoons vanilla**
- **2 10-ounce packages frozen strawberries in light syrup, thawed**
- **1 tablespoon lemon juice**
- **Fresh strawberries, halved (optional)**

1. In a small saucepan, stir together sugar, cornstarch, and lemon peel. Stir in milk. Cook and stir until thickened and bubbly. Cook and stir for 2 minutes more. Stir in vanilla. Cover; chill about 1 hour or until cold.

2. In a food processor, combine strawberries in light syrup and lemon juice. Cover; process until smooth.

3. Stir strawberry mixture into chilled milk mixture. Pour into a 1½- to 2-quart ice cream freezer. Freeze according to manufacturer directions. Pack the mixture into a freezer container. Cover and freeze about 3 hours or until firm. If desired, serve with fresh strawberries. Makes 12 (½-cup) servings.

Honey-Apricot Frozen Yogurt

To save even more carbs, choose a yogurt that's made with a sugar substitute. Pictured on *page 132*.

PER SERVING: 93 cal., 1 g total fat (1 g sat. fat), 4 mg chol., 50 mg sodium, 18 g carb., 1 g fiber, 4 g pro. Exchanges: 0.5 other carb., 0.5 milk. Carb choices: 1.

- **3 cups pitted and finely chopped fresh apricots* or nectarines**
- **4 cups vanilla low-fat yogurt**
- **2 tablespoons honey**
- **Sliced fresh apricots and/or nectarines (optional)**

1. In a large food processor, combine half of the chopped apricots, all of the yogurt, and honey. Cover and process until smooth. (For smaller processors, process in two batches.)

2. Pour the apricot mixture into a 2-quart freezer container. Stir in remaining chopped apricots. Cover and freeze about 4 hours or until firm.

3. Chill the mixer bowl for a heavy stand electric mixer. Spoon frozen mixture into chilled bowl. Beat with the mixer on medium speed until slightly fluffy, starting slowly and gradually increasing the speed. Return to freezer container. Cover and freeze about 6 hours or until firm.

4. Let frozen yogurt stand at room temperature for 20 minutes before serving. If desired, serve with sliced apricots. Makes 12 (½-cup) servings.

***Note:** If you can't find fresh apricots, drain and use three 15-ounce cans unpeeled apricot halves in light syrup.

Mango Mousse

This light, impressive dessert is one you can turn to when you are entertaining or for a special meal.

PER SERVING: 97 cal., 2 g total fat (2 g sat. fat), 0 mg chol., 12 mg sodium, 17 g carb., 0 g fiber, 3 g pro. Exchanges: 1 carb., 0.5 fat. Carb choices: 1.

- **2 cups mango nectar**
- **1 envelope unflavored gelatin**
- **2 teaspoons lime juice**
- **5 drops yellow food coloring (optional)**
- **1 drop red food coloring (optional)**
- **½ of an 8-ounce container frozen light whipped dessert topping, thawed**
- **1 ripe mango, seeded, peeled, and cut into thin strips**
- **Fresh mint leaves (optional)**

Having diabetes can take the fun out of enjoying sweets. But you don't have to forgo desserts altogether. Just choose wisely. Reach for these good-for-you treats the next time you want to celebrate. We've lightened them all—just for you.

Very Berry Sorbet

If fresh berries aren't in season, use purchased frozen blueberries and raspberries instead.

PER SERVING: 67 cal., 0 g total fat, 0 mg chol., 7 mg sodium, 16 g carb., 3 g fiber, 1 g pro. Exchanges: 0.5 carb., 0.5 fruit. Carb choices: 1.

2 cups fresh blueberries, frozen*
2 cups fresh raspberries, frozen*
½ cup cold water
¼ cup frozen pineapple-orange-banana juice concentrate or citrus beverage concentrate
Fresh blueberries and/or raspberries (optional)

1. In a large bowl, combine frozen berries, the water, and frozen concentrate. Place half of the mixture in a food processor. Cover and process until almost smooth. Repeat with remaining mixture. Serve immediately with additional blueberries and/or raspberries, if desired. Makes 6 (½-cup) servings.

Make-Ahead Directions: Prepare as directed. Transfer mixture to a 1½-quart freezer container. Cover and freeze about 4 hours or until firm. Use within 2 days.

***Note:** To freeze, place berries in a single layer on a pan; place in the freezer. Transfer frozen berries to a freezer container; seal, label, and store for up to 12 months.

Rocky Road Parfaits

Sugar-free pudding and light whipped dessert topping trim and slim these chocolaty treats.

PER SERVING: 162 cal., 6 g total fat (2 g sat. fat), 2 mg chol., 386 mg sodium, 21 g carb., 1 g fiber, 7 g pro. Exchanges: 0.5 fat-free milk, 1 carb., 1 fat. Carb choices: 1.5.

1 4-serving-size package sugar-free instant chocolate or chocolate fudge pudding mix
2 cups fat-free milk
½ cup frozen light whipped dessert topping, thawed
¼ cup unsalted peanuts, coarsely chopped
¼ cup tiny marshmallows
Chocolate curls (optional)

1. Prepare pudding mix according to package directions using the fat-free milk. Remove ¾ cup of the pudding and place in a small bowl; fold in whipped topping until combined.

2. Divide the remaining plain chocolate pudding among four 6-ounce glasses or dessert dishes. Top with chocolate-dessert topping mixture. Let stand for 5 to 10 minutes or until set.

3. Just before serving, sprinkle each parfait with peanuts and marshmallows. If desired, garnish with chocolate curls. Makes 4 servings.

Make-Ahead Directions: Prepare as directed through Step 2. Cover and chill parfaits for up to 24 hours. Serve as directed in Step 3.

Black Forest Trifle

If fresh dark cherries aren't available, don't worry. Frozen cherries will also work in this dessert.

PER SERVING: 102 cal., 1 g total fat (1 g sat. fat), 1 mg chol., 110 mg sodium, 22 g carb., 1 g fiber, 3 g pro. Exchanges: 1.5 carb. Carb choices: 1.5.

1 8-ounce package no-sugar-added low-fat chocolate cake mix
1 4-serving-size package sugar-free instant chocolate pudding mix
2 cups fat-free milk
1 pound fresh dark sweet cherries, pitted, or one 16-ounce package frozen unsweetened pitted dark sweet cherries, thawed and well-drained
2 cups frozen fat-free whipped dessert topping, thawed
Unsweetened cocoa powder (optional)

Black Forest Trifle

1. Prepare cake mix according to package directions in a 13×9×2-inch baking pan. Cool in pan on a wire rack for 10 minutes; remove from pan. Cut into 1-inch pieces.

2. Meanwhile, prepare pudding mix according to package directions using the 2 cups fat-free milk. Cover; chill about 30 minutes or until set.

3. In a 3-quart trifle bowl or glass bowl, layer half of the cake cubes, half of the cherries, half of the chocolate pudding, and half of the whipped topping. Repeat the layers. If desired, sprinkle with cocoa powder. Makes 16 (⅔-cup) servings.

Make-Ahead Directions: Prepare trifle as directed. Cover and chill for up to 4 hours.

Kona Trifle Cups

Kona, Hawaii's prized coffee, is featured in this dessert. But any strong-brewed coffee will do.

PER SERVING: 141 cal., 6 g total fat (3 g sat. fat), 56 mg chol., 87 mg sodium, 17 g carb., 0 g fiber, 4 g pro. Exchanges: 1 carb., 1.5 fat. Carb choices: 1. PER SERVING WITH SUBSTITUTE: same as above, except 106 cal., 8 g carb. Exchanges: 0.5 carb. Carb choices: 0.5.

½ of a 3-ounce package ladyfingers (12 halves), cubed
¼ cup strong-brewed Kona or other coffee
¼ of an 8-ounce package reduced-fat cream cheese (Neufchâtel), softened
⅓ cup light dairy sour cream
3 tablespoons sugar or sugar substitute* equivalent to 3 tablespoons sugar
1 teaspoon vanilla
2 to 3 teaspoons fat-free milk

1. Divide ladyfinger cubes among four 4- to 6-ounce dessert dishes or custard cups. Drizzle ladyfinger cubes with coffee. Set aside.

2. In a small bowl, stir together cream cheese, sour cream, sugar, and vanilla. Beat with a wire whisk until smooth. Stir in enough of the milk to make desired consistency. Spoon cream cheese mixture onto ladyfinger cubes. Cover and chill for 1 hour. Makes 4 servings.

***Sugar Substitutes:** Choose from Equal Spoonful or packets or Sweet'N Low bulk or packets. Follow package directions to use product amount equivalent to 3 tablespoons sugar.

Summer Berry Panna Cotta

This luscious dessert will enchant everyone with its beauty and seemingly rich flavor.

PER SERVING: 115 cal., 0 g total fat, 0 mg chol., 62 mg sodium, 22 g carb., 4 g fiber, 2 g pro. Exchanges: 0.5 fruit, 1 carb. Carb choices: 1.

2 tablespoons water
1¼ teaspoons unflavored gelatin
1½ cups fat-free half-and-half
2 tablespoons sugar or sugar substitute* equivalent to 2 tablespoons sugar
1 teaspoon finely shredded lemon peel
1 teaspoon vanilla
1 tablespoon raspberry liqueur or sugar-free raspberry preserves
1 tablespoon orange liqueur or orange juice
4 cups fresh berries (such as raspberries, sliced strawberries, blueberries, and/or blackberries)
Fresh mint sprigs (optional)

1. In a medium bowl, for panna cotta, combine the water and gelatin; let stand about 5 minutes or until softened (mixture will be very thick).

2. In a small saucepan, combine half-and-half, 1 tablespoon of the sugar, and lemon peel. Cook and stir over medium heat just until bubbling. Remove from heat; stir into gelatin mixture until gelatin is dissolved. Stir in vanilla. Cover and chill for 3 to 6 hours or until soft set.

3. Meanwhile, in a large bowl, stir together remaining 1 tablespoon sugar, raspberry liqueur, and orange liqueur. Gently fold in berries.

4. Whisk gelatin mixture until smooth. Spoon about 3 tablespoons panna cotta into each glass. Divide the berry mixture among six dessert glasses or dishes. If desired, garnish with mint. Makes 6 servings (about ¼ cup panna cotta and ⅔ cup fruit each).

***Sugar Substitutes:** Choose from Splenda granular or Sweet'N Low bulk or packets. Follow package directions to use product amounts equivalent to the sugar.

No-Bake Chocolate Swirl Cheesecake

Low-fat cream cheese and sour cream keep this lovely cheesecake light and luscious.

PER SERVING: 184 cal., 11 g total fat (7 g sat. fat), 29 mg chol., 232 mg sodium, 15 g carb., 1 g fiber, 7 g pro. Exchanges: 1 carb., 2 fat. Carb choices: 1.

PER SERVING WITH SUBSTITUTE: same as above, except 168 cal., 11 g carb.

½ cup crushed graham crackers
2 tablespoons butter, melted
1 envelope unflavored gelatin
¾ cup fat-free milk
2 8-ounce packages reduced-fat cream cheese (Neufchâtel), softened
1 8-ounce package fat-free cream cheese, softened
1 8-ounce carton fat-free dairy sour cream
⅓ cup sugar or sugar substitute* equivalent to ⅓ cup sugar
2 teaspoons vanilla
4 ounces semisweet chocolate, melted and cooled
Chocolate curls (optional)

1. For crust, in a bowl, combine cracker crumbs and butter until moistened. Press onto the bottom of an 8-inch springform pan (may not cover completely). Cover and chill.

2. For filling, in a saucepan, sprinkle gelatin into milk; let stand for 5 minutes. Stir over low heat until gelatin is dissolved. Remove from heat; cool for 15 minutes.

3. In a bowl, beat cream cheeses until smooth. Beat in sour cream, sugar, and vanilla; slowly beat in gelatin mixture. Divide in half. Stir chocolate into one portion.

4. Spoon half of the chocolate filling onto chilled crust; spread evenly. Carefully spoon half of the white filling onto chocolate in small mounds. Using a narrow spatula or knife, swirl chocolate and white fillings. Top with remaining chocolate and white fillings, spreading each evenly. Swirl again. Cover and chill for 6 to 24 hours.

5. To serve, loosen cheesecake from pan; remove pan side. If desired, top with chocolate curls. Makes 16 servings.

***Sugar Substitutes:** Choose from Splenda granular, Equal Spoonful or packets, or Sweet'N Low bulk or packets. Follow package directions to use product amount equivalent to ⅓ cup sugar.

No-Bake Chocolate Swirl Cheesecake

Glazed Tropical Fruit Pie

You can use peaches or nectarines instead of the mango.

PER SERVING: 185 cal., 7 g total fat (4 g sat. fat), 16 mg chol., 104 mg sodium, 29 g carb., 2 g fiber, 2 g pro. Exchanges: 1 fruit, 1 carb., 1.5 fat. Carb choices: 2.

- **1 cup pineapple-orange juice**
- **1 tablespoon cornstarch**
- **2 cups 1-inch pieces seeded, peeled mango**
- **2 cups 1-inch pieces seeded, peeled papaya**
- **1½ cups half-slices peeled kiwifruit**
- **1 recipe Graham Cracker Pie Shell (see recipe, below) or 1 purchased 9-inch graham cracker crumb pie shell***
- **Frozen light whipped dessert topping, thawed (optional)**

1. In a small saucepan, combine juice and cornstarch; cook and stir until thickened and bubbly. Cook and stir for 2 minutes more. Transfer to a large bowl. Cover surface with plastic wrap; cool for 30 minutes.

2. Divide juice mixture among three small bowls. In each bowl, fold one fruit into juice mixture. Spoon fruit into pie shell, arranging as desired. Cover and chill for 3 to 4 hours. If desired, serve with dessert topping. Makes 10 servings.

Graham Cracker Pie Shell: Preheat oven to 375°F. In a small saucepan, melt ⅓ cup butter. Stir in ¼ cup sugar. Add 1¼ cups finely crushed graham crackers; mix well. Press evenly onto bottom and up side of a 9-inch pie plate. Bake for 4 to 5 minutes or until edge is light brown. Cool on a wire rack.

***Test Kitchen Tip:** To more easily cut the pie using the purchased graham cracker pie shell, preheat oven to 375°F. Brush the pie shell with a slightly beaten egg white; bake for 5 minutes. Cool on a wire rack before filling.

Berry Pie with Creamy Filling

Yogurt cheese, which is used in the pie filling, takes 24 hours to make. Keep that in mind when you are planning to make this gorgeous pie.

PER SERVING: 160 cal., 4 g total fat (2 g sat. fat), 10 mg chol., 87 mg sodium, 27 g carb., 3 g fiber, 5 g pro. Exchanges: 1 fruit, 1 carb., 0.5 fat. Carb choices: 2.

- **1 16-ounce carton plain fat-free or low-fat yogurt***
- **2 tablespoons powdered sugar**
- **½ teaspoon vanilla**
- **¾ cup low-calorie cranberry-raspberry drink**
- **1 tablespoon cornstarch**
- **1 recipe Zwieback Crust (see recipe, below)**
- **6 cups fresh raspberries, blackberries, blueberries, and/or halved strawberries**
- **Fresh mint and/or Lemon Cream (see *below*) (optional)**

1. For yogurt cheese, set a sieve over a large bowl; line with three layers of 100-percent-cotton cheesecloth. Spoon in yogurt. Cover with plastic wrap and chill for 24 hours. Discard the liquid from the yogurt cheese. In a medium bowl, combine yogurt cheese, powdered sugar, and vanilla. Cover and chill until ready to use.

2. For glaze, in a saucepan, stir together fruit drink and cornstarch. Cook and stir over medium heat until thickened and bubbly; cook and stir for 2 minutes more. Transfer to a bowl. Cover surface with plastic wrap; let stand at room temperature for 1 to 2 hours or until cool.

3. Spread yogurt cheese mixture into Zwieback Crust. In a large bowl, gently toss berries and cooled glaze. Spoon onto yogurt mixture. Cover; chill for 3 to 6 hours. If desired, garnish with mint and/or serve with Lemon Cream. Makes 10 servings.

***Test Kitchen Tip:** For yogurt cheese, choose a yogurt that contains no gums, gelatin, or fillers because they may prevent the whey from separating from the curd.

Zwieback Crust: Preheat oven to 350°F. Coat a 9-inch pie plate with nonstick cooking spray. In a medium bowl, combine 1⅓ cups finely crushed zwieback (about 17 slices) and 2 tablespoons packed brown sugar. Add 1 slightly beaten egg white and 2 tablespoons melted butter; stir until mixed. Press evenly onto bottom and up side of pie plate. Bake for 10 to 12 minutes or until edge is brown. Cool on a wire rack.

Lemon Cream: In a bowl, combine 1½ cups thawed light whipped dessert topping and ¾ teaspoon finely shredded lemon peel.

(10 keys to success)

To keep your diabetes in check, follow these guidelines.

1. **Follow** a meal plan—it takes away the guesswork.
2. **Measure** and weigh foods—estimate when eating out or on special occasions.
3. **Limit** starches and balance meals with nonstarchy vegetables.
4. **Eat** vegetables and fruits daily—three to four servings of each.
5. **Enjoy** most anything, but watch your portion sizes (especially with desserts!).
6. **Avoid** munching throughout the day.
7. **Bake,** broil, or grill foods—avoid fried foods.
8. **Cut down** on desserts overall—but have a small serving on special occasions.
9. **Split** a meal when eating out and order an extra side salad instead of fries.
10. **Keep** food, exercise, and blood glucose records.

Berry Pie with Creamy Filling

Incredible Apple Tart

(ending on a sweet note)

When preparing desserts, experiment using the minimum amount of sweetener possible to get the desired results and the flavor you like. Make the sweetness of sugar work harder by magnifying it with vanilla or spices, such as cinnamon and cloves. And you don't always have to use bar chocolate either. When a recipe calls for unsweetened chocolate and when it is feasible, substitute unsweetened cocoa powder, a lower-fat alternative to bar chocolate. For each ounce of bar chocolate, stir together 3 tablespoons of cocoa powder and 1 tablespoon water.

Incredible Apple Tart

Jonathan, Rome Beauty, or Winesap apples are great choices for this tart.

PER SERVING: 153 cal., 9 g total fat (5 g sat. fat), 21 mg chol., 149 mg sodium, 15 g carb., 2 g fiber, 4 g pro. Exchanges: 1 carb., 1.5 fat. Carb choices: 1.

- **1 recipe Pecan Tart Crust (see recipe, below)**
- **Nonstick cooking spray**
- **½ of an 8-ounce package reduced-fat cream cheese (Neufchâtel)**
- **⅓ cup light dairy sour cream**
- **1 egg white**
- **4 tablespoons low-sugar orange marmalade**
- **¼ teaspoon ground cardamom**
- **2 medium red cooking apples, cored and very thinly sliced***

1. Preheat oven to 375°F. Pat Pecan Tart Crust dough evenly onto the bottom and up the sides of a lightly greased 9-inch tart pan with a removable bottom. Line pastry with a double thickness of foil that has been coated with cooking spray. Bake pastry for 4 minutes. Remove foil. Bake for 3 minutes more. Cool completely on a wire rack.

2. Meanwhile, in a medium bowl, combine cream cheese, sour cream, egg white, 2 tablespoons of the orange marmalade, and the cardamom; beat with electric mixer until smooth. Spread cream cheese mixture onto cooled crust.

3. Arrange apple slices in two concentric rings on top of the cream cheese mixture in tart pan, overlapping slices slightly. Cover top of tart with foil.

4. Bake for 35 minutes. Uncover and bake for 10 to 15 minutes more or until crust is golden and apples are just tender.

5. Place remaining 2 tablespoons orange marmalade in a small microwave-safe bowl. Cover; microwave on 50 percent power (medium) for 10 seconds. Stir; microwave about 10 seconds more or until melted. Brush onto apples. Serve tart slightly warm or cool. Makes 12 servings.

Pecan Tart Crust: In a small bowl, combine ⅔ cup quick-cooking rolled oats, ½ cup white whole wheat flour or whole wheat flour, and ¼ cup toasted ground pecans. In a large bowl, combine half of an 8-ounce package reduced-fat cream cheese (Neufchâtel) and 2 tablespoons softened butter; beat with an electric mixer on medium to high speed for 30 seconds. Add 2 tablespoons packed brown sugar, 1 teaspoon finely shredded orange peel, ¼ teaspoon baking soda, and ⅛ teaspoon salt; beat until mixed. Beat in as much of the oat mixture as you can with the mixer. Using a wooden spoon, stir in any remaining oat mixture. If necessary, cover and chill for 30 to 60 minutes or until the dough is easy to handle.

***Test Kitchen Tip:** If you have a mandoline, use it to slice the apples about ⅛ inch thick.

Easy Blueberry Tarts

The addition of cayenne pepper is optional but will give these tarts a hint of spice and distinct Mexican flair.

PER SERVING: 131 cal., 1 g total fat (0 g sat. fat), 0 mg chol., 93 mg sodium, 29 g carb., 3 g fiber, 2 g pro. Exchanges: 1 carb., 1 fruit. Carb choices: 2.

- **Nonstick cooking spray**
- **3 tablespoons sugar**
- **1 teaspoon cornstarch**
- **⅛ teaspoon cayenne pepper (optional)**
- **¼ cup water**
- **1 cup fresh blueberries**
- **1 cup fresh raspberries**
- **¼ teaspoon ground cinnamon**
- **4 sheets frozen phyllo dough (9×14-inch rectangles), thawed**

1. Preheat oven to 375°F. Lightly coat four 4×2×½-inch rectangular tart pans that have removable bottoms with cooking spray; set aside. In a small saucepan, stir together 2 tablespoons of the sugar, cornstarch, and, if desired, cayenne pepper. Stir in the water and half of the blueberries. Cook and stir over medium heat until mixture is thickened and bubbly. Fold in remaining blueberries and the raspberries; set aside.

2. In a small bowl, stir together remaining 1 tablespoon sugar and cinnamon. Place one sheet of phyllo on cutting board. Lightly coat with cooking spray; sprinkle with about 1 teaspoon sugar mixture. Repeat layering with remaining phyllo and sugar mixture, ending with cooking spray. With a sharp knife, cut phyllo stack in half lengthwise and crosswise, forming four rectangles. Ease rectangles into prepared tart pans.

3. Bake for 8 minutes or until phyllo is golden brown. Cool slightly; remove shells from pans. Spoon filling into shells just before serving. Serve warm or cool. Makes 4 servings.

Walnut Berry-Cherry Crisp

The golden crisp topper boasts walnuts, flaxseeds, and oats.

PER SERVING: 171 cal., 9 g total fat (1 g sat. fat), 0 mg chol., 3 mg sodium, 23 g carb., 3 g fiber, 3 g pro. Exchanges: 0.5 fruit, 0.5 starch, 0.5 carb., 1.5 fat. Carb choices: 1.5.

PER SERVING WITH SUBSTITUTE: 158 cal., 20 g carb. Carb choices: 1.

- **2 cups fresh or frozen blueberries**
- **2 cups frozen unsweetened pitted tart red cherries**
- **4 tablespoons all-purpose flour**
- **1 tablespoon honey**
- **2 tablespoons flaxseeds, toasted***
- **½ cup rolled oats**
- **⅓ cup chopped walnuts**
- **2 tablespoons packed brown sugar or brown sugar substitute* equivalent to 2 tablespoons brown sugar**
- **2 tablespoons canola oil**

1. Thaw fruit, if frozen (do not drain). Preheat oven to 375°F. In a medium bowl, combine blueberries, cherries, 2 tablespoons of the flour, and the honey. Divide blueberry mixture among eight 6-ounce ramekins or custard cups, or spoon blueberry mixture into a 1½-quart casserole.

2. Place toasted flaxseeds in a spice grinder and pulse until ground to a fine powder. In a medium bowl, stir together ground flaxseeds, oats, walnuts, the remaining 2 tablespoons flour, brown sugar, and oil. Sprinkle onto fruit mixture.

3. Bake for 15 to 20 minutes for ramekins or custard cups or 25 to 30 minutes for casserole or until topping is golden and fruit mixture is bubbly around edges. Serve warm. Makes 8 (about ½-cup) servings.

***Test Kitchen Tip:** To toast flaxseeds, place in a small dry skillet over medium heat. Cook and stir until the seeds are fragrant and begin to pop.

****Sugar Substitutes:** Choose from Sweet'N Low Brown or Sugar Twin Granulated Brown. Follow package directions to use product amount equivalent to 2 tablespoons brown sugar.

Walnut Berry-Cherry Crisp

Raspberry-Peach Crisp

A crunchy oat topping adds a little extra fiber and toasted flavor.

PER SERVING: 159 cal., 4 g total fat (2 g sat. fat), 8 mg chol., 23 mg sodium, 31 g carb., 4 g fiber, 3 g pro. Exchanges: 1 fruit, 0.5 carb., 0.5 starch, 0.5 fat. Carb choices: 2.

PER SERVING WITH SUBSTITUTES: same as above, except 137 cal., 25 g carb. Carb choices: 1.5.

- **4 cups sliced fresh peaches or frozen unsweetened peach slices, thawed**
- **2 tablespoons granulated sugar or sugar substitute* equivalent to 2 tablespoons granulated sugar**
- **1 tablespoon quick-cooking tapioca**
- **2 tablespoons sugar-free red raspberry preserves**
- **⅔ cup quick-cooking rolled oats**
- **2 tablespoons whole wheat flour**
- **2 tablespoons packed brown sugar or brown sugar substitute* equivalent to 2 tablespoons brown sugar**
- **½ teaspoon ground cinnamon**
- **2 tablespoons butter**
- **Vanilla low-fat frozen yogurt (optional)**

1. Preheat oven to 375°F. For fruit filling, thaw fruit, if frozen; do not drain. In a large bowl, combine peach slices, granulated sugar, tapioca, and raspberry preserves. Place fruit mixture in a 2-quart square baking dish.

Raspberry-Peach Crisp

2. For topping, in a medium bowl, stir together oats, whole wheat flour, brown sugar, and cinnamon. Using a pastry blender, cut in the butter until crumbly. Sprinkle topping onto fruit in dish.

3. Bake for 45 to 50 minutes or until the fruit filling is bubbly. Cool on a wire rack; serve warm. If desired, serve with frozen yogurt. Makes 8 (½-cup) servings.

***Sugar Substitutes:** Choose from Splenda granular or Sweet'N Low bulk or packets for the granulated sugar. Choose from Sweet'N Low Brown, Sugar Twin Granulated Brown, or Splenda Brown Sugar Blend for the brown sugar. Follow package directions to use equivalent product amounts.

Double Chocolate Brownies

Oatmeal-Applesauce Cake

Serve this hearty cake as a dessert or a snack.

PER SERVING: 157 cal., 4 g total fat (2 g sat. fat), 9 mg chol., 121 mg sodium, 28 g carb., 2 g fiber, 3 g pro. Exchanges: 2 carb., 0.5 fat. Carb choices: 2.

Nonstick cooking spray
1 cup all-purpose flour
1 cup whole wheat pastry flour
⅔ cup quick-cooking rolled oats
2 teaspoons baking powder
1½ teaspoons ground cinnamon
½ teaspoon baking soda
¼ teaspoon salt
¼ teaspoon ground nutmeg
⅔ cup packed brown sugar
⅓ cup butter, softened
¼ cup refrigerated or frozen egg product, thawed, or 1 egg
2 teaspoons vanilla
1¾ cups unsweetened applesauce
¾ cup mixed dried fruit bits or raisins
½ cup quick-cooking rolled oats
3 tablespoons toasted wheat germ
2 tablespoons packed brown sugar
Fresh raspberries (optional)

1. Preheat oven to 350°F. Lightly coat a 13×9×2-inch baking pan with nonstick cooking spray; set aside.
2. In a medium bowl, use a fork to stir together all-purpose flour, whole wheat pastry flour, the ⅔ cup oats, baking powder, cinnamon, baking soda, salt, and nutmeg. Set the flour mixture aside.
3. In a large bowl, combine the ⅔ cup brown sugar and the butter. Beat with an electric mixer on medium speed until mixed. Beat in egg and vanilla. Alternately add flour mixture and applesauce to beaten mixture, beating after each addition just until combined. Stir in fruit bits. Spread batter into the prepared pan.
4. For topping, in a small bowl, combine the ½ cup oats, the wheat germ, and the 2 tablespoons brown sugar. Sprinkle mixture onto batter; press lightly into batter.
5. Bake for 25 to 30 minutes or until a toothpick inserted near center comes out clean. Cool in pan on a wire rack. Cut into squares to serve. If desired, top each square with raspberries. Makes 20 servings.

Double Chocolate Brownies

Semisweet chocolate and cocoa powder give twice the flavor with half the fat.

PER BROWNIE: 113 cal., 4 g total fat (2 g sat. fat), 8 mg chol., 37 mg sodium, 17 g carb., 0 g fiber, 1 g pro. Exchanges: 1 carb., 1 fat. Carb choices: 1.

Nonstick cooking spray
¼ cup butter or margarine
⅔ cup granulated sugar
½ cup cold water
1 teaspoon vanilla
1 cup all-purpose flour
¼ cup unsweetened cocoa powder
1 teaspoon baking powder
¼ cup miniature semisweet chocolate pieces
Sifted powdered sugar (optional)

1. Preheat oven to 350°F. Lightly coat the bottom of a 9×9×2-inch baking pan with cooking spray, being careful not to coat sides of pan.
2. In a medium saucepan, melt butter; remove from heat. Stir in granulated sugar, the water, and vanilla. Add flour, cocoa powder, and baking powder; stir until combined. Stir in chocolate pieces.
3. Pour batter into prepared pan. Bake for 15 to 18 minutes or until a toothpick inserted near the center comes out clean. Cool in pan on a wire rack.
4. Before serving, if desired, sprinkle with powdered sugar. Cut into 16 bars. Makes 16 brownies.

Oatmeal-Applesauce Cake

Nutty Carrot Cake Bars

A small amount of oil (which has no saturated fat, unlike butter) is what makes these bars moist.

PER BAR: 121 cal., 7 g total fat (2 g sat. fat), 5 mg chol., 64 mg sodium, 12 g carb., 1 g fiber, 3 g pro. Exchanges: 1 carb., 1 fat. Carb choices: 1.
PER BAR WITH SUBSTITUTE: same as above, except 102 cal., 7 g carb. Exchanges: 0.5 carb. Carb choices: 0.5.

Nonstick cooking spray
¾ cup all-purpose flour
½ cup sugar or sugar substitute* equivalent to ½ cup sugar
¼ cup whole wheat flour
1½ teaspoons pumpkin pie spice
1 teaspoon baking powder
⅛ teaspoon salt
1 cup finely shredded carrots
¾ cup chopped walnuts or pecans, toasted
⅓ cup refrigerated or frozen egg product, thawed, or 3 egg whites, lightly beaten
¼ cup cooking oil
¼ cup fat-free milk
1 recipe Fluffy Cream Cheese Frosting (see recipe, below)

1. Preheat oven to 350°F. Line a 9×9×2-inch baking pan with foil, extending over edges. Lightly coat foil with cooking spray. Set aside.

2. In a medium bowl, combine all-purpose flour, sugar, whole wheat flour, pumpkin pie spice, baking powder, and salt. Add carrots, ½ cup of the nuts, eggs, oil, and milk. Stir just until combined. Spread evenly in pan.

3. Bake for 15 to 18 minutes or until a toothpick inserted near center comes out clean. Cool bars in pan on a wire rack.

4. Using the edges of the foil, lift uncut bars out of pan. Spread top evenly with Fluffy Cream Cheese Frosting. Sprinkle with remaining ¼ cup nuts. Cut into bars. Store, covered, in the refrigerator for up to 3 days. Makes 20 bars.

Fluffy Cream Cheese Frosting: Thaw ½ cup frozen light whipped dessert topping. In a medium bowl, beat half of an 8-ounce package softened reduced-fat cream cheese (Neufchâtel) with an electric mixer on medium speed until smooth. Beat in ¼ cup vanilla low-fat yogurt until smooth. Fold in thawed whipped topping.

***Sugar Substitute:** Use Sweet'N Low bulk or packets. Follow package directions to use product amount equivalent to ½ cup sugar.

Nutty Carrot Cake Bars

Peanut-Apple Crunch Balls

Wetting your hands makes the peanut mixture easier to shape for these no-bake cereal treats.

PER BALL: 94 cal., 6 g total fat (2 g sat. fat), 1 mg chol., 76 mg sodium, 9 g carb., 1 g fiber, 2 g pro. Exchanges: 0.5 carb., 1 fat. Carb choices: 0.5.

⅓ cup chunky peanut butter
¼ cup 68 percent vegetable oil spread
2 tablespoons honey
1 cup rice and wheat cereal flakes, crushed slightly
1 cup bran flakes, crushed slightly
⅓ cup finely snipped dried apples
2 tablespoons finely chopped peanuts
⅛ teaspoon apple pie spice
2 ounces white baking chocolate (with cocoa butter), chopped
¼ teaspoon shortening

1. In a medium saucepan, combine peanut butter, vegetable oil spread, and honey. Cook over low heat just until melted and nearly smooth, whisking constantly. Stir in rice and wheat cereal flakes, bran flakes, apples, peanuts, and apple pie spice until mixed.

2. Divide cereal mixture into 18 portions. Using slightly wet hands, shape the cereal mixture into balls. Let stand on a waxed-paper-lined baking sheet about 15 minutes or until firm.

3. In a small saucepan, combine white chocolate and shortening. Cook over low heat until melted, stirring constantly. Drizzle balls with melted white chocolate. Let stand about 15 minutes or until white chocolate is set (if necessary, chill balls until white chocolate is firm). Makes 18 balls.

(fruit is fine)

All fruit—raw, cooked, canned, frozen, dried, or juiced—contains fruit sugar, or fructose. However, raw fruit has a higher fiber content, which has been associated with a lower rise in blood glucose. For example, a small apple and ½ cup of apple juice both contain 15 grams of carbohydrates. The apple offers 3 grams of dietary fiber, while the juice contains none. Raw fruits can also be more satisfying, but remember to watch portion sizes—a bigger fruit equals more sugar.

Whole Grain Chocolate Chip Cookies

Kids of all ages will love these hearty chippers.

PER COOKIE: 94 cal., 5 g total fat (1 g sat. fat), 9 mg chol., 19 mg sodium, 11 g carb., 1 g fiber, 2 g pro. Exchanges: 1 carb., 1 fat. Carb choices: 1.
PER COOKIE WITH SUBSTITUTE: same as above, except 87 cal., 9 g carb. Exchanges: 0.5 carb. Carb choices: 0.5.

- **1 cup whole wheat flour**
- **1 cup regular rolled oats**
- **½ cup barley flour**
- **½ cup oat bran**
- **¼ cup wheat bran**
- **3 tablespoons nonfat dry milk powder**
- **1½ teaspoons baking powder**
- **¼ teaspoon baking soda**
- **2 eggs or ½ cup refrigerated or frozen egg product, thawed**
- **1 cup sugar or sugar substitute blend* equivalent to 1 cup sugar**
- **¾ cup cooking oil**
- **1 teaspoon vanilla**
- **½ cup miniature semisweet chocolate pieces**
- **½ cup chopped walnuts**
- **¼ cup unsweetened shredded coconut (optional)**

1. Preheat oven to 375°F. In a large bowl, stir together wheat flour, oats, barley flour, oat bran, wheat bran, dry milk powder, baking powder, and baking soda.

2. In a bowl, beat eggs. Stir in sugar, oil, and vanilla; stir into flour mixture. Stir in chocolate, walnuts, and, if desired, coconut. Drop dough by rounded teaspoons 2 inches apart onto an ungreased cookie sheet.

3. Bake for 8 to 10 minutes or until edges are set and bottoms are light brown. Transfer to a wire rack; let cool. Makes about 48 cookies.

***Sugar Substitutes:** Choose Splenda Sugar Blend for Baking or Equal Sugar Lite. Follow package directions to use product amount equivalent to 1 cup sugar.

Whole Grain Chocolate Chip Cookies

managing your diabetes

Understanding diabetes gives you a better chance of controlling it and preventing complications. It pays to learn all you can, then develop a plan that fits your lifestyle.

An estimated 21 million people in the United States, or 7 percent of the U.S. population, have diabetes, according to the Centers for Disease Control and Prevention. An additional 54 million Americans have pre-diabetes—indicating an increased risk of developing diabetes. If you're one of them, remember that you—not your doctor, dietitian, or other health professional—play the most important role in staying healthy.

Define Your Diabetes

Your health-care team will work with you to develop a personalized diabetes management plan, consisting of healthful foods, physical activity, and, if necessary, the medication that's right for you and your type of diabetes (type 1, type 2, or gestational).

Type 1 diabetes: In this type, the pancreas doesn't produce insulin, so people with type 1 diabetes must take insulin. A typical treatment plan begins with an individualized meal plan, guidelines for physical activity, and blood glucose testing. Insulin therapy is then planned around lifestyle and eating patterns.

Type 2 diabetes: In type 2 diabetes, either the pancreas doesn't produce enough insulin or the body doesn't properly respond to insulin, so too much glucose remains in the blood. Many people control type 2 diabetes by following a specially designed meal plan and engaging in regular physical activity. The right plan can help people reach and attain a desirable weight, plus healthy blood glucose, blood cholesterol, and blood pressure levels. As the disease progresses, treatment may expand to include oral medications, oral medications with insulin, or insulin alone.

Gestational diabetes: This type develops only during pregnancy. Women who've had gestational diabetes have a higher risk of developing type 2 diabetes.

Develop Your Meal Plan

Adhering to a healthful meal plan is one of the most important measures you can take to control your blood glucose. Work with a dietitian to design a meal plan that reflects your individual needs and preferences. Your meal plan should also:

- Include fruits, vegetables, and whole grains.
- Reduce the amount of saturated fat and cholesterol you eat.
- Minimize the amount of salt or sodium you eat.
- Incorporate a moderate amount of sugar because some sugar can be part of a healthful diabetes meal plan.
- Help you maintain or achieve an ideal weight.

Follow Your Meal Plan

As you start following your meal plan, you'll see that it gives you some flexibility regarding what, how much, and when you eat, but you have to be comfortable with the foods it suggests. It will guide you in eating appropriate amounts of three major nutrients—carbohydrates, protein, and fat—at the right times. Your meal plan will be nutritionally balanced, allowing you to get the vitamins, minerals, and fiber your body needs. And if you need to lose weight, it will indicate how many calories you should consume every day in order to lose the extra pounds at a realistic pace.

(monitor your blood glucose)

Whether you have type 1 or type 2 diabetes, it's important to test your blood glucose, especially if you're taking insulin shots or oral medication. Usually you test blood glucose before each meal. Your health-care providers will teach you how to measure your blood glucose with a simple finger-prick test, as well as how to adjust your food intake, physical activity, and/or medication when your blood glucose is too high or too low. Your health-care providers will help you set blood glucose goals. For example, the American Diabetes Association suggests a target for fasting or before meals is 90 to 130 milligrams/deciliter. At two hours after the start of a meal, the goal is less than 180 milligrams/deciliter. Your A1C level (the average amount of glucose in the blood over the last few months) should be less than 7. To keep your blood glucose at a healthy level, follow these five important guidelines:

- Eat about the same amount of food each day.
- Eat meals and snacks at about the same times each day.
- Do not skip meals or snacks.
- Take medicines at the same times each day.
- Do physical activity at about the same times each day.

Your meal plan can be simple, especially if you use a proven technique to keep track of what you're eating. Two well-known meal-planning systems for diabetes are diabetic exchanges and carbohydrate counting. Your dietitian may suggest one or the other. To help you follow either system, every recipe in this book provides nutrition information, including the number of exchanges and carb choices in each serving. (Turn to page 153 to see how to use this information.)

Track the Exchanges
Exchange Lists for Meal Planning outlines a system designed by the American Diabetes Association and the American Dietetic Association. To use the exchange system, your dietitian will work with you to develop a pattern of food exchanges—or a meal plan—suited to your specific needs. You'll be able to keep track of the number of exchanges from various food groups that you eat each day. Tally those numbers and match the total to the daily allowance set in your meal plan. (For more information, see www.diabetes.org.)

Count Carbohydrates
Carbohydrate counting is the method many diabetes educators prefer for keeping tabs on what you eat. It makes sense because the carbohydrate content of foods has the greatest effect on blood glucose levels. If you focus on carbohydrates, you can eat a variety of foods and still control your blood glucose.

When counting carbohydrates, you can tally the number of grams you eat each day. Or you can count the number of carbohydrate choices, which allows you to work with smaller numbers. We offer both numbers with our recipes.

(low-calorie sweeteners)

There's no need to dump low-calorie sweeteners just because sugar is safer than once thought. Sweeteners are "free foods" in your meal plan—and that's a good thing! They make foods taste sweet, they have no calories, and they won't raise your blood glucose levels. The following sweeteners are accepted by the Food and Drug Administration as safe to eat: aspartame (Equal and NutraSweet), acesulfame potassium (Sweet One), saccharin (Sweet'N Low and Sugar Twin), and sucralose (Splenda).

Basic carbohydrate counting relies on eating about the same amount of carbohydrates at the same times each day to keep blood glucose levels in your target range. It's a good meal-planning method if you have type 2 diabetes and take no daily oral diabetes medications or take one to two shots of insulin per day.

Advanced carbohydrate counting is a more complex method than the basic system of carbohydrate counting. It's designed for individuals who take multiple daily insulin injections or use an insulin pump. With advanced carbohydrate counting, you have to balance the amount of carbohydrates you consume with the insulin you take. You estimate the amount of carbohydrates you'll be eating and adjust your mealtime insulin dose based on your recommended insulin-to-carbohydrate ratio. To learn how to follow advanced carbohydrate counting, seek the assistance of a registered dietitian or certified diabetes educator.

The Carbohydrate Question

Although the calories from fat, protein, and carbohydrates all affect your blood glucose level, carbohydrates affect it the most. So why not just avoid carbohydrates altogether? While carbohydrates may be the main nutrient that raises blood glucose levels, you shouldn't cut them from your diet. Foods that contain carbohydrates are among the most healthful available—vegetables, fruits, whole grains, and low- or nonfat dairy foods. Eliminating these foods could compromise your health.

(be a sugar sleuth)

Knowing the different forms of sugar can make life sweeter when you're reading labels and recipes. Sugar content is included in the total grams we list for carbohydrates in recipes.

- Sucrose appears in table sugar, molasses, beet sugar, brown sugar, cane sugar, powdered sugar, raw sugar, turbinado, and maple syrup.
- Other "-ose" sugars include glucose (or dextrose), fructose, lactose, and maltose. Fructose and sugar alcohols affect blood glucose less than sucrose, but large amounts of fructose may increase blood fat levels.
- Sugar alcohols such as sorbitol, xylitol, maltitol, mannitol, lactitol, and erythritol should only be eaten in moderation because they can cause diarrhea, gas, and cramping.

How Sweet It Is

For many years, people with diabetes were told to shun sugar because it was thought that sugar caused blood glucose to soar out of control. So they diligently wiped sugary foods and sugar out of their diets, hoping to stabilize their blood glucose levels. Today, more than a dozen studies have shown sugars in foods don't cause blood glucose to spike any higher or faster than starches, such as those in potatoes and bread. The American Diabetes Association's recommendations on sugar now state "scientific evidence has shown that the use of sucrose (table sugar) as part of the meal plan does not impair blood glucose control in individuals with type 1 or type 2 diabetes."

It is important to note, however, that sugar is not a "free food." It still contains calories and offers no nutritional value beyond providing energy. So when you eat foods that contain sugar, they have to replace other carbohydrate-rich foods in your meal plan. Carbohydrates you eat contain a healthful amount of vitamins, minerals, and fiber. So it's a good idea to focus on whole grains and vegetables for your carbohydrates rather than sugar. Talk to your dietitian to determine a healthful way to include a moderate amount of sugar in your meal plan. Or you can also sweeten foods with sugar substitutes (see "Low-Calorie Sweeteners," page 151).

Stay Involved and Informed

Eating healthfully, exercising, and monitoring blood glucose levels help keep diabetes in check—all easier to do if you follow the plans you've developed with your health-care providers. Update them on your progress and request changes if something isn't working. And stay informed about diabetes by going to www.diabeticlivingonline.com to sign up for our e-mail newsletter. You're the one who can monitor your progress day by day.

(using our nutrition information)

At the top of every one of our recipes, you'll see the nutrition information listed for each serving. You'll find the amount of calories (cal.), total fat, saturated fat (sat. fat), cholesterol (chol.), sodium, total carbohydrates (carb.), fiber, and protein (pro.). In addition, you'll find the number of diabetic exchanges for each serving and the number of carbohydrate choices, in case you prefer those methods to keep track of what you're eating.

PER SERVING: 134 cal., 9 g total fat (1 g sat. fat), 0 mg chol., 60 mg sodium, 14 g carb., 4 g fiber, 2 g pro. Exchanges: 0.5 fruit, 1 vegetable, 2 fat. Carb choices: 1.

Interpreting the Numbers
Use our nutrition analyses to keep track of the nutritional value of the foods you eat, following the meal plan you and your dietitian have decided is right for you. Refer to that plan to see how a recipe fits the number of diabetic exchanges or carbohydrate choices you're allotted for each day. When you try a recipe, jot down our nutrition numbers to keep a running tally of what you're eating, remembering your daily allowances. At the end of each day, see how your numbers compare to your plan.

Diabetic Exchanges
The exchange system allows you to choose from a variety of items within several food groupings. Those groupings include starch, fruit, fat-free milk, carbohydrates, nonstarchy vegetables, meat and meat substitutes, fat, and free foods. To use the diabetic exchange system with our recipes, follow your plan's recommendations on the number of servings you should select from each exchange group in a day.

Carbohydrate Counting
Our recipes help you keep track of carbohydrates in two ways—tallying grams of carbohydrates and the number of carbohydrate choices. For counting grams, add the amounts of total carbohydrates to your running total for the day. For carbohydrate choices, one choice equals 15 grams of carbohydrates. For example, a sandwich made with two slices of bread is 2 carbohydrate choices. The benefit of this system is that you're keeping track of small numbers.

Calculating Method
To calculate our nutrition information and offer flexibility in our recipes, we've made some decisions about what's included in our analyses and what's not. We follow these guidelines when we analyze recipes that list ingredient options or serving suggestions:

- When ingredient choices appear (such as yogurt or sour cream), we use the first one mentioned for the analysis.
- When an ingredient is listed as optional, such as a garnish or a suggested serve-along, we don't include it in our nutrition analysis.
- When we offer a range in the number of servings, we use the smaller number.
- For marinades, we assume most of it is discarded.

recipe index

A–B

C

D–F

G–J

K–M

N–O

P–R

33

96

V–Z

metric information

The charts on this page provide a guide for converting measurements from the U.S. customary system, which is used throughout this book, to the metric system.

Product Differences

Most of the ingredients called for in the recipes in this book are available in most countries. However, some are known by different names. Here are some common American ingredients and their possible counterparts:

- All-purpose flour is enriched, bleached or unbleached white household flour. When self-rising flour is used in place of all-purpose flour in a recipe that calls for leavening, omit the leavening agent (baking soda or baking powder) and salt.
- Baking soda is bicarbonate of soda.
- Cornstarch is cornflour.
- Golden raisins are sultanas.
- Light-colored corn syrup is golden syrup.
- Powdered sugar is icing sugar.
- Sugar (white) is granulated, fine granulated, or castor sugar.
- Vanilla or vanilla extract is vanilla essence.

Volume and Weight

The United States traditionally uses cup measures for liquid and solid ingredients. The chart below shows the approximate imperial and metric equivalents. If you are accustomed to weighing solid ingredients, the following approximate equivalents will be helpful.

- 1 cup butter, castor sugar, or rice = 8 ounces = ½ pound = 250 grams
- 1 cup flour = 4 ounces = ¼ pound = 125 grams
- 1 cup icing sugar = 5 ounces = 150 grams

Canadian and U.S. volume for a cup measure is 8 fluid ounces (237 ml), but the standard metric equivalent is 250 ml.

1 British imperial cup is 10 fluid ounces.

In Australia, 1 tablespoon equals 20 ml, and there are 4 teaspoons in the Australian tablespoon.

Spoon measures are used for smaller amounts of ingredients. Although the size of the tablespoon varies slightly in different countries, for practical purposes and for recipes in this book, a straight substitution is all that's necessary. Measurements made using cups or spoons always should be level unless stated otherwise.

Common Weight Range Replacements

Imperial / U.S.	Metric
½ ounce	15 g
1 ounce	25 g or 30 g
4 ounces (¼ pound)	115 g or 125 g
8 ounces (½ pound)	225 g or 250 g
16 ounces (1 pound)	450 g or 500 g
1¼ pounds	625 g
1½ pounds	750 g
2 pounds or 2¼ pounds	1,000 g or 1 Kg

Oven Temperature Equivalents

Fahrenheit Setting	Celsius Setting*	Gas Setting
300°F	150°C	Gas Mark 2 (very low)
325°F	160°C	Gas Mark 3 (low)
350°F	180°C	Gas Mark 4 (moderate)
375°F	190°C	Gas Mark 5 (moderate)
400°F	200°C	Gas Mark 6 (hot)
425°F	220°C	Gas Mark 7 (hot)
450°F	230°C	Gas Mark 8 (very hot)
475°F	240°C	Gas Mark 9 (very hot)
500°F	260°C	Gas Mark 10 (extremely hot)
Broil	Broil	Grill

*Electric and gas ovens may be calibrated using celsius. However, for an electric oven, increase celsius setting 10 to 20 degrees when cooking above 160°C. For convection or forced air ovens (gas or electric), lower the temperature setting 25°F/10°C when cooking at all heat levels.

Baking Pan Sizes

Imperial / U.S.	Metric
9×1½-inch round cake pan	22- or 23×4-cm (1.5 L)
9×1½-inch pie plate	22- or 23×4-cm (1 L)
8×8×2-inch square cake pan	20×5-cm (2 L)
9×9×2-inch square cake pan	22- or 23×4.5-cm (2.5 L)
11×7×1½-inch baking pan	28×17×4-cm (2 L)
2-quart rectangular baking pan	30×19×4.5-cm (3 L)
13×9×2-inch baking pan	34×22×4.5-cm (3.5 L)
15×10×1-inch jelly roll pan	40×25×2-cm
9×5×3-inch loaf pan	23×13×8-cm (2 L)
2-quart casserole	2 L

U.S. / Standard Metric Equivalents

⅛ teaspoon = 0.5 ml
¼ teaspoon = 1 ml
½ teaspoon = 2 ml
1 teaspoon = 5 ml
1 tablespoon = 15 ml
2 tablespoons = 25 ml
¼ cup = 2 fluid ounces = 50 ml
⅓ cup = 3 fluid ounces = 75 ml
½ cup = 4 fluid ounces = 125 ml
⅔ cup = 5 fluid ounces = 150 ml
¾ cup = 6 fluid ounces = 175 ml
1 cup = 8 fluid ounces = 250 ml
2 cups = 1 pint = 500 ml
1 quart = 1 litre